WILLIAMS-SONOMA

FOODMADEFAST
asian

RECIPES

Farina Wong Kingsley

GENERAL EDITOR

Chuck Williams

PHOTOGRAPHY

Bill Bettencourt

Oxmoor
House®

contents

20 MINUTES START TO FINISH

10 cashew chicken

13 dry-fried string beans with pork

14 beef with ginger & caramelized onions

17 beef sukiyaki with noodles

18 sesame-crusted tuna with greens

21 chicken with peanut sauce

22 chile-garlic prawns

25 crab fried rice

26 tangerine beef & snow peas

29 seared salmon with basil

30 spicy tofu with peas

33 hot & sour soup with pork

34 japanese pork katsu

37 sweet & sour panfried sole

38 thai red curry beef

41 salt & pepper shrimp

42 spring vegetable stir-fry

45 sea bass with ginger & green onions

30 MINUTES START TO FINISH

48 caramelized halibut with bok choy

51 eggplant, portobello & chicken stir-fry

52 vietnamese beef noodle salad

55 beef & broccoli

56 lemongrass pork stir-fry

59 five-spice chicken noodle soup

60 grilled hoisin pork chops
   & asparagus

63 braised soy-ginger chicken & bok choy

64 miso-glazed scallops with asian slaw

67 vegetable chow mein

68 thai green curry shrimp

71 braised salmon & shiitakes

72 thai pumpkin & chicken curry

15 MINUTES HANDS-ON TIME

76 shanghai noodles with pork

79 grilled vietnamese chicken

80 rice with chicken, mushrooms & chard

83 curried chickpea & potato stew

84 roasted honey-soy pork tenderloin

87 curried cauliflower & chicken stew

88 yellow chicken curry

91 indian braised lamb

92 sichuan braised pork with eggplant

95 the smarter cook

103 the well-stocked kitchen

108 index

about this book

Nowadays, we are more and more concerned about what we eat. We want to sit down to meals that are both delicious and good for us. But our lives are also more hectic than ever before, leaving us less time to cook. The dishes of Asia, which offer remarkable variety in style and flavor, are the ideal solution for today's busy home cook.

Food Made Fast *Asian* is designed to put wholesome, tasty, Asian-inspired meals on the dinner table in record time and with minimal effort. Recipes such as Salt & Pepper Shrimp and Tangerine Beef & Snow Peas take no more than 20 minutes from pantry to table, while Shanghai Noodles with Pork and Curried Chickpea & Potato Stew require less than 15 minutes of hands-on time. Most of the recipes can be served as one-dish suppers, accompanied by only rice or noodles, which means less time in the kitchen and more time enjoying home-cooked meals.

Chuck

20 minutes
start to finish

cashew chicken

Soy sauce, 3 tablespoons

Rice wine or dry sherry, 1 tablespoon

Ginger, 2 teaspoons grated

Skinless, boneless chicken thighs, 1 lb (500 g), cut into bite-sized pieces

Worcestershire sauce, 1 teaspoon

Asian sesame oil, 1 teaspoon

Sugar, ½ teaspoon

Cornstarch (cornflour), ¼ teaspoon

Corn or peanut oil, 3 tablespoons

Green (spring) onions, 2, chopped

Salted roasted cashews, 1 cup (5½ oz/170 g)

Steamed rice, for serving

SERVES 4

1 Marinate the chicken
In a large bowl, stir together 2 tablespoons of the soy sauce, the wine, and the ginger. Stir in the chicken to coat evenly and set aside for 15 minutes.

2 Make the sauce
In a small bowl, combine 2 tablespoons water, the remaining 1 tablespoon soy sauce, and the Worcestershire sauce, sesame oil, sugar, and cornstarch and stir to dissolve the sugar and cornstarch.

3 Stir-fry the chicken
Heat a wok or large frying pan over high heat until very hot and add 2 tablespoons of the corn oil. Remove the chicken from the marinade, draining it well, and discard the marinade. Add the chicken to the wok and stir-fry until opaque, about 3 minutes. Using a slotted spoon, transfer the chicken to a bowl. Return the pan to medium heat and add the remaining 1 tablespoon corn oil. Add the green onions and stir-fry for about 10 seconds until fragrant. Return the chicken to the pan and add the cashews. Give the sauce a quick stir, add to the pan, and stir until the sauce thickens slightly, 1–2 minutes. Serve with the rice.

cook's tip

For a quick and easy side dish, separate 1 lb (500 g) broccoli into small florets. Bring a pot of salted water to a boil, add the broccoli, and cook just until bright green and tender-crisp, about 3 minutes. Drain well, place in a dish, drizzle lightly with soy sauce and chile or sesame oil, toss, and serve.

dry-fried string beans with pork

1 Parboil the green beans
Bring a large pot of water to a boil. Add the beans, parboil for 2 minutes, and drain into a colander. Place under running cold water to halt the cooking. Pat the beans dry.

2 Make the sauce
In a small bowl, combine the beef broth, soy sauce, rice vinegar, cornstarch, and sugar and stir to dissolve the cornstarch and sugar.

3 Stir-fry the beans
Heat a wok or large frying pan over high heat until very hot and add the oil. Add the pork and stir-fry until no longer pink, about 2 minutes. Add the ginger, garlic, green onion, and chile and stir-fry for about 10 seconds until fragrant. Add the green beans and stir to mix. Give the sauce a quick stir, add to the pan, and stir-fry until the beans are heated through and the sauce thickens, about 1 minute. Serve with the rice.

Green beans, 1 lb (500 g), trimmed and cut into bite-sized pieces

Beef broth, 1/2 cup (4 fl oz/125 ml)

Soy sauce, 3 tablespoons

Rice vinegar, 1 tablespoon

Cornstarch (cornflour), 1 teaspoon

Sugar, 1/2 teaspoon

Corn or peanut oil, 2 tablespoons

Ground (minced) pork, 1/4 lb (125 g)

Ginger, 1 tablespoon minced

Garlic, 2 cloves, minced

Green (spring) onion, 1, chopped

Red or green jalapeño chile, 1 small, seeded and minced

Steamed rice, for serving

SERVES 4

beef with ginger & caramelized onions

Beef tenderloin or sirloin,
1½ lb (750 g), cut across the
grain into thin strips

Soy sauce, 5 tablespoons

Rice wine or dry sherry,
2 tablespoons

Worcestershire sauce,
2 tablespoons

Asian sesame oil,
2 teaspoons

Sugar, ½ teaspoon

Cornstarch (cornflour),
½ teaspoon

Freshly ground pepper

Corn or peanut oil,
2 tablespoons

Yellow onion, 1 large, thinly
sliced

**Orange or yellow bell
pepper (capsicum),** 1,
seeded and sliced (optional)

Ginger, 1 tablespoon grated

Red pepper flakes
(optional)

Steamed rice, for serving

SERVES 4

1 Marinate the beef
In a large bowl, combine the beef, 1 tablespoon of the
soy sauce, and the wine and mix to coat the beef evenly. Set
aside for 10 minutes.

2 Make the sauce
In a small bowl, combine 4 tablespoons water, the
remaining 4 tablespoons soy sauce, and the Worcestershire
sauce, sesame oil, sugar, cornstarch, and 1 teaspoon of
pepper and stir to dissolve the sugar and cornstarch.

3 Stir-fry the vegetables
Heat a wok or large frying pan over high heat until
very hot and add 1 tablespoon of the corn oil. Add the onion
and bell pepper, if using, and stir-fry until caramelized, about
10 minutes. Using a slotted spoon, transfer the onion mixture
to a plate. Return the pan to high heat and add the remaining
1 tablespoon oil. Add the ginger and stir-fry until fragrant, about
10 seconds. Add the beef and stir-fry just until it begins to
brown and is still rare in the center, about 1 minute. Return
the onion mixture to the pan. Give the sauce a quick stir,
add to the pan, and stir until the sauce thickens slightly, about
10 seconds. Sprinkle with red pepper flakes to taste, if desired.
Serve with the rice.

cook's tip

Look for fresh ginger that feels firm and heavy for its size and has smooth, shiny, pale skin. Use a vegetable peeler or the edge of a spoon to remove the thin skin before cutting as directed in a recipe. You may use a variety of tools to grate ginger, including a rasp-style grater; a specialized flat ceramic grater with tiny, sharp rasps; or the finest holes on a box grater-shredder.

cook's tip

The meat must be very thinly
sliced for this dish. Ask your
butcher to slice it for you with a
slicing machine, or put it into
the freezer for at least 30 minutes
or up to 1 hour and then slice
it yourself. Firming it up in the
freezer makes cutting very thin,
uniform slices easier.

beef sukiyaki with noodles

1 Make the braising liquid
In a bowl, combine ¼ cup (2 fl oz/60 ml) water and the soy sauce, mirin, sake, and sugar and stir to dissolve the sugar.

2 Stir-fry the vegetables
Heat a wok or large frying pan over high heat until very hot and add the oil. Add the yellow onion and stir-fry just until tender, about 3 minutes. Add the mushrooms and stir-fry for 1 minute. Add the cabbage and stir-fry just until the cabbage wilts and the mushrooms have softened, about 2 minutes.

3 Braise the vegetables and beef
Reduce the heat to medium, pour the braising liquid over the vegetables, and bring to a low simmer. Stir in the noodles and beef, and simmer for about 3 minutes. Transfer to a serving dish, garnish with the green onions, and serve.

Low-sodium soy sauce, 1 cup (8 fl oz/250 ml)

Mirin, ½ cup (4 fl oz/ 125 ml)

Sake, ½ cup (4 fl oz/125 ml)

Sugar, 2 tablespoons

Corn or peanut oil, 2 tablespoons

Yellow onion, 1, thinly sliced

Shiitake mushrooms, ½ lb (8 oz/250 g), stems discarded and caps thinly sliced

Napa cabbage, ½ large head, shredded

Cellophane noodles, 6 oz (185 g), soaked in hot water to cover for 15 minutes and drained

Beef sirloin, 1 lb (500 g), very thinly sliced across the grain

Green (spring) onions, 2, thinly sliced

SERVES 4

17

sesame-crusted tuna with greens

Ginger, 1 tablespoon grated

Green (spring) onions,
2, thinly sliced

Rice vinegar, 2 tablespoons

Soy sauce, 1 tablespoon

Fresh orange juice,
2 tablespoons

Honey, 1 teaspoon (optional)

Asian sesame oil,
1 teaspoon

Corn or peanut oil,
4 tablespoons (2 fl oz/60 ml)
plus 1 teaspoon

Orange, 1

**Sushi-grade ahi tuna
steaks,** 1 lb (500 g), 1 inch
(2.5 cm) thick

Salt

Sesame seeds,
2 tablespoons

**Mixed baby salad greens
or arugula (rocket) leaves,**
5 oz (155 g)

SERVES 4

1 **Make the vinaigrette**
In a small bowl, whisk together the ginger, green onions, vinegar, soy sauce, orange juice, honey, sesame oil, and 2 tablespoons of the corn oil. Set aside. To segment the orange, cut a slice off the top and bottom, then stand the orange upright. Following the contour of the orange, slice downward to remove the peel and pith, then cut the sections free into a large bowl.

2 **Sear the tuna**
Heat a stove-top grill pan or large nonstick frying pan over high heat until very hot. Meanwhile, rub the tuna on both sides with the 1 teaspoon corn oil. Sprinkle a pinch of salt on each side of the tuna. Spread the sesame seeds evenly on a plate. Lay the tuna on top of the sesame seeds and press firmly so that the seeds adhere, coating evenly. Turn the tuna and repeat on the other side. Add the remaining 2 tablespoons oil to the pan and then add the tuna. Sear, turning once, until crisp and golden brown on both sides, about 2 minutes on each side. Transfer the tuna to a plate and refrigerate for 10 minutes.

3 **Assemble the salad**
Slice the tuna across the grain into pieces ½ inch (12 mm) thick. Place the baby greens in the bowl with the orange segments, drizzle with half of the vinaigrette, and toss to coat evenly. Mound the salad on a platter or plates, top with the tuna, and drizzle with the remaining vinaigrette.

cook's tip

Many kinds of dried Asian noodles need to be reconstituted in hot water before they can be eaten. Place the noodles in a large bowl, add hot water to cover, place a plate on top of the noodles to keep them submerged, and set aside for 15 minutes.

chicken with peanut sauce

1 Make the peanut sauce
In a blender, combine ¼ cup (2 fl oz/60 ml) warm water and the peanut butter, soy sauce, rice vinegar, sesame oil, chile paste, and sugar. Process until a smooth sauce forms. If the sauce is too thick, add up to 1 tablespoon warm water.

2 Cook the noodles
Bring a large pot of water to a boil. Plunge the reconstituted noodles into the water for 5 seconds and drain immediately. Pour the noodles back into the warm pot, add the spinach and corn oil, and toss gently to distribute the ingredients evenly.

3 Assemble and serve
In a bowl, toss the shredded chicken with half of the peanut sauce. Transfer the noodles to a large bowl or platter and scatter the chicken on top. Garnish with the peanuts and cilantro. Pass the remaining peanut sauce at the table.

Creamy peanut butter, 3 tablespoons

Soy sauce, 3 tablespoons

Rice vinegar, 3 tablespoons

Asian sesame oil, 2 tablespoons

Chile paste, ½ teaspoon

Sugar, ¼ teaspoon

Dried rice noodles or rice vermicelli, ½ lb (250 g), soaked in hot water to cover for 15 minutes and drained

Baby spinach, ½ lb (250 g)

Corn or peanut oil, 1 tablespoon

Cooked shredded chicken, homemade or rotisserie, 1½ cups (9 oz/280 g)

Roasted peanuts, 1 tablespoon chopped

Fresh cilantro (fresh coriander), 3 tablespoons chopped

SERVES 4

21

chile-garlic prawns

Soy sauce, 6 tablespoons
(3 fl oz/90 ml)

Rice vinegar, ¼ cup (2 fl oz/
60 ml)

Asian sesame oil,
4 teaspoons

Ketchup, ¼ cup (2 oz/60 g)

Sugar, 2 teaspoons

Cornstarch (cornflour),
2 teaspoons

Corn or peanut oil,
3 tablespoons

Tiger prawns, 2 lb (1 kg),
peeled and deveined

Ginger, 2 tablespoons minced

Garlic, 4 cloves, minced

**Red or green jalapeño
chile,** 1, seeded and minced

Green (spring) onions,
6, thinly sliced

Steamed rice, for serving

SERVES 4

1 Make the sauce
In a small bowl, combine 6 tablespoons water and the soy sauce, vinegar, sesame oil, ketchup, sugar, and cornstarch and stir to dissolve the sugar and cornstarch.

2 Stir-fry the prawns
Heat a wok or large frying pan over high heat until very hot and add 2 tablespoons of the corn oil. Add the prawns and sear, turning once, until browned on both sides, about 1 minute on each side. Using a slotted spoon, transfer the prawns to a bowl. Return the pan to high heat and add the remaining 1 tablespoon oil. Add the ginger, garlic, chile, and two-thirds of the green onions and stir-fry for about 10 seconds until fragrant. Give the sauce a quick stir, add to the pan, and stir until it begins to bubble. Immediately add the prawns and stir-fry until the prawns are opaque throughout and the sauce has thickened slightly, about 1 minute. Transfer to a platter, garnish with the remaining green onions, and serve with the rice.

cook's tip

For a simple side dish, heat 1 tablespoon corn oil in a wok over high heat. Add 1 clove garlic, smashed, and 2 slices ginger. Stir-fry for

about 10 seconds. Add 1 lb (500 g) sugar snap peas, stir-fry 1–2 minutes, then add 3 tablespoons water and 1–2 tablespoons soy sauce. Cover and cook over medium heat until the peas are tender-crisp, about 1 minute. Drizzle with sesame oil and serve.

cook's tip

To save time, include an extra
order of rice when you take out
Chinese food or make a double
batch one night, reserving half for
later use. Microwave the rice just
until warm and use it for making
fried rice.

crab
fried rice

1 Make the sauce
In a small bowl, combine the soy sauce, vinegar, sesame oil, sugar, and a pinch of white pepper and stir to dissolve the sugar.

2 Stir-fry the rice
Heat a wok or large nonstick frying pan over high heat until very hot and add the corn oil. Add the ginger, garlic, and green onions and stir-fry for about 5 seconds until fragrant. Add the rice and continue to stir-fry until the rice is hot, about 5 minutes. Create a small well in the middle of the rice, exposing the bottom of the pan. Add the eggs to the well and immediately stir-fry to incorporate them into the rice. Once the eggs are cooked through, add the crabmeat, peas, and sauce and stir-fry until well combined and heated through, 2–3 minutes. Transfer to a platter and serve.

Soy sauce, 1/4 cup (2 fl oz/ 60 ml)

Rice vinegar, 1 1/2 tablespoons

Asian sesame oil, 1 teaspoon

Sugar, 1/2 teaspoon (optional)

White pepper

Corn or peanut oil, 2 tablespoons

Ginger, 1 tablespoon minced

Garlic, 3 cloves, minced

Green (spring) onions, 3, thinly sliced

Steamed white rice, 4 cups (1 1/4 lb/625 g), warm

Eggs, 2, beaten

Fresh lump crabmeat, 1/2 lb (250 g), picked over for shell fragments

Frozen petite peas, 1 cup (5 oz/155 g)

SERVES 4

tangerine beef & snow peas

Beef sirloin or skirt steak,
1 lb (500 g), cut against the
grain into thin strips

Soy sauce, 2 tablespoons

**Fresh tangerine or orange
juice,** 3 tablespoons

Rice wine or dry sherry,
2 tablespoons

Hoisin sauce, 2 tablespoons

Asian sesame oil,
1 teaspoon

Cornstarch (cornflour),
½ teaspoon

Corn or peanut oil,
3 tablespoons

Garlic, 2 cloves, minced

Ginger, 1 tablespoon grated

Snow peas (mangetouts),
¼ lb (125 g), trimmed, strings
removed, and cut in half

Steamed rice, for serving

SERVES 4

1 Marinate the beef
In a large bowl, combine the beef and soy sauce, mix
well, and set aside for 10 minutes.

2 Make the sauce
In a small bowl, combine 2 tablespoons water, and the
tangerine juice, wine, hoisin sauce, sesame oil, and cornstarch
and stir to dissolve the cornstarch.

3 Stir-fry the beef
Heat a wok or large frying pan over high heat until
very hot and add 2 tablespoons of the corn oil. Add the garlic,
ginger, and beef and stir-fry just until the beef is browned,
about 2 minutes. Using a slotted spoon, transfer the meat to
a bowl. Return the pan to high heat and add the remaining
1 tablespoon oil. Add the snow peas and stir-fry until tender,
about 2 minutes. Give the sauce a quick stir, add to the pan,
and stir until the sauce thickens slightly, about 10 seconds.
Return the meat to the pan and stir-fry until heated through,
about 1 minute. Serve with the rice.

cook's tip

Jasmine rice is a long-grain variety that originated in Thailand. It is prized for its aromatic character, mildly nutty flavor, and long, slender kernels that steam up fluffy and slightly sticky. The finest jasmine rice still comes from northern Thailand. Look for it in well-stocked supermarkets and Chinese and Southeast Asian grocery stores.

seared salmon with basil

1 Make the chile-garlic paste

In a blender, combine 1 tablespoon water and the garlic, chile, green onions, and cilantro. Add the basil and process until a paste forms.

2 Make the sauce

In a small bowl, combine 2 tablespoons water and the fish sauce, lime juice, and sugar and stir to dissolve the sugar. Heat a small frying pan over medium heat until hot and add 2 tablespoons of the oil. Add the chile-garlic paste and sauté until very fragrant, 1–2 minutes. Stir in the fish sauce mixture and simmer for 2 minutes to blend the flavors. Keep warm.

3 Sear the salmon

Season each salmon fillet with a pinch each of salt and pepper. Heat a large frying pan over high heat until very hot and add the remaining 1 tablespoon oil. Add the salmon and sear, turning once, until golden brown on the outside and still slightly rare in the center, about 2 minutes on each side. Transfer the salmon to a platter or dinner plates and drizzle with the warm sauce. Serve with the rice.

Garlic, 2 cloves, coarsely chopped

Green jalapeño chile, 1, coarsely chopped

Green (spring) onions, 3, chopped

Fresh cilantro (fresh coriander), 3 tablespoons chopped

Fresh basil, preferably Thai, ¼ cup (⅓ oz/10 g), chopped

Asian fish sauce, 2 tablespoons

Fresh lime juice, from ½ lime

Sugar, 1 teaspoon

Corn or peanut oil, 3 tablespoons

Salmon fillets, 4, about 1½ lb (750 g) total weight

Salt and freshly ground pepper

Steamed rice, for serving

SERVES 4

spicy tofu with peas

Oyster sauce, ¼ cup
(2 fl oz/60 ml)

Soy sauce, ¼ cup (2 fl oz/
60 ml)

Rice vinegar, ¼ cup (2 fl oz/
60 ml)

**Sriracha hot sauce or
tomato paste,** 2 teaspoons

Asian sesame oil,
2 tablespoons

Sugar, 2 teaspoons

Cornstarch (cornflour),
1 teaspoon

Corn or peanut oil,
¼ cup (2 fl oz/60 ml)

Ginger, 2 tablespoons minced

Garlic, 4 cloves, minced

Firm tofu, 2 lb (1 kg),
drained and cut into bite-sized
cubes

Frozen petite peas, 1 cup
(5 oz/155 g)

Steamed rice, for serving

SERVES 4

1 Make the sauce

In a small bowl, combine ¼ cup (2 fl oz/60 ml) water
and the oyster sauce, soy sauce, vinegar, Sriracha hot sauce,
sesame oil, sugar, and cornstarch and stir to dissolve the sugar
and cornstarch.

2 Stir-fry the tofu

Heat a wok or large frying pan over high heat until
very hot and add the corn oil. Add the ginger and garlic and
stir-fry for about 5 seconds until fragrant. Reduce the heat
to medium, pour in the sauce, and add the tofu. Stir-fry gently
until the sauce thickens slightly, about 1 minute. Add the
peas and continue to cook until heated through, about 1 minute
longer. Serve with the rice.

cook's tip

Tofu is sold in three basic types, silken, soft, and firm, according to how much water is in the tofu. Custardlike silken tofu, a specialty of Japan, is traditionally eaten with just a sprinkle of soy sauce and green (spring) onions, but is also good for making sauces and puréed dishes. Soft tofu is a common addition to soups and steamed dishes, while firm tofu is ideal for stir-fries.

cook's tip

This soup may be prepared a day in advance. Let cool, transfer to an airtight container, and store in the refrigerator; reheat just before serving. You may also freeze the soup for up to 3 months. Thaw in the refrigerator.

hot & sour soup with pork

1 Make the soup seasoning
In a small bowl, combine the soy sauce, Worcestershire sauce, vinegar, sesame oil, chile paste, cornstarch, and sugar and stir to dissolve the cornstarch and sugar.

2 Cook the soup
Heat a large, heavy saucepan over high heat until hot and add the corn oil. Add the ginger and all but 1 tablespoon of the green onions and sauté for about 5 seconds until fragrant. Add the pork and mushrooms and sauté until the pork is just opaque, about 1 minute. Pour in the chicken broth, bring to a boil, and then reduce the heat to low. Give the soup seasoning a quick stir, add to the soup, stir well, and simmer, stirring occasionally, until the soup begins to thicken slightly, about 5 minutes. Ladle into bowls, garnish with the reserved green onions, and serve.

Soy sauce, 6 tablespoons (3 fl oz/90 ml)

Worcestershire sauce, 3 tablespoons

Rice vinegar, 2 tablespoons

Asian sesame oil, 1 tablespoon

Chile paste, ½ teaspoon

Cornstarch (cornflour), 1 tablespoon

Sugar, 1 teaspoon (optional)

Corn or peanut oil, 2 tablespoons

Ginger, 2 tablespoons grated

Green (spring) onions, 3, thinly sliced

Pork tenderloin or boneless loin, ½ lb (250 g), thinly sliced across the grain and cut into small strips

Shiitake mushrooms or button mushrooms, 6 oz (185 g), stems discarded and caps thinly sliced

Chicken broth, 6 cups (48 fl oz/1.5 l)

SERVES 4

33

japanese pork katsu

Soy sauce, 1 tablespoon

Mirin or sake, 1 tablespoon

Worcestershire sauce, 1 tablespoon

Ketchup, 3 tablespoons

Hot mustard, ½ teaspoon

Pork cutlets, 4, 1½ lb (750 g) total weight

Egg, 1

Flour, 2 tablespoons

Panko or plain fine dried bread crumbs, 1 cup (4 oz/125 g)

Salt and freshly ground pepper

Corn or peanut oil, ¼ cup (2 fl oz/60 ml)

Steamed rice, for serving

SERVES 4

1 **Make the dipping sauce**
In a bowl, stir together 1 tablespoon hot water and the soy sauce, mirin, Worcestershire sauce, ketchup, and mustard.

2 **Prepare the pork**
One at a time, place the pork cutlets between 2 sheets of waxed paper or plastic wrap and pound with a meat pounder until ¼ inch (6 mm) thick. In a shallow bowl, lightly beat the egg. Spread the flour and _panko_ on 2 separate plates. Season the flour with a pinch each of salt and pepper. Just before frying, season the cutlets with salt on both sides and then dip them first in the flour, then in the egg, and finally in the _panko_, coating evenly each time and pressing the _panko_ with your fingertips so it adheres.

3 **Panfry the pork**
Heat a large nonstick frying pan over medium-high heat until just hot and add the oil. Add the cutlets and fry, turning once, until golden brown on both sides and just opaque at the center, about 5 minutes on each side. Transfer the cutlets to paper towels to drain briefly, then cut across the grain into strips ½ inch (12 mm) thick. Serve with the dipping sauce and rice.

cook's tip

Pork katsu, a staple Japanese
dish, is traditionally served with
a simple shredded cabbage
salad. Soak 3 cups (9 oz/280 g)
shredded cabbage in cold water
for 15 minutes, then drain well.
Transfer to a bowl and toss with
a squeeze of lemon or a drizzle
or rice wine vinegar. Serve
alongside the pork and rice.

cook's tip

If you cannot find *panko*—delicate, Japanese bread crumbs—you can easily make and store your own bread crumbs. Process slices of good-quality, day-old white bread in a food processor. Spread on a baking sheet and dry in a 250°F (120°C) oven for 10–15 minutes. Process again for finer crumbs. Store in an airtight container in the freezer for up to 2 months.

sweet & sour
panfried sole

1 Make the sauce
In a small saucepan over medium heat, stir together ¼ cup (2 fl oz/60 ml) water and the vinegar, soy sauce, ketchup, sesame oil, sugar, and cornstarch. Bring to a simmer and cook, stirring occasionally, until the sauce thickens, about 1 minute. Keep warm.

2 Prepare the fish
In a shallow bowl, lightly beat the egg. Spread the flour and *panko* on 2 separate plates. Season the flour with a pinch each of salt and pepper. Just before frying, season the sole fillets with salt on both sides and then dip them first in the flour, then in the egg, and finally in the *panko*, coating evenly each time and pressing the *panko* with your fingertips so it adheres.

3 Panfry the fish
Heat a large nonstick frying pan over high heat until just hot and add the oil. Add the fish and fry, turning once, until golden brown on both sides, 3–4 minutes on each side. Transfer the fillets to paper towels to drain briefly, then serve with the sauce.

Rice vinegar, 1 tablespoon

Soy sauce, 1 tablespoon

Ketchup, 3 tablespoons

Asian sesame oil, 1 teaspoon

Sugar, 1 tablespoon

Cornstarch (cornflour), ½ teaspoon

Egg, 1

Flour, 2 tablespoons

***Panko* or plain fine dried bread crumbs,** 1 cup (4 oz/125 g)

Salt and freshly ground pepper

Petrale or Dover sole fillets, 4, about 1½ lb (750 g) total weight

Corn or peanut oil, 3 tablespoons

SERVES 4

thai red curry beef

Unsweetened coconut milk, 1 cup (8 fl oz/250 ml)

Asian fish sauce, ¼ cup (2 fl oz/60 ml)

Light brown sugar, 2 teaspoons firmly packed

Fresh lime juice, from ½ lime

Corn or peanut oil, 4 tablespoons (2 fl oz/60 ml)

Yellow onion, 1, thinly sliced

Green or red bell pepper (capsicum), 1, seeded and thinly sliced lengthwise

Thai red curry paste, 1 tablespoon

Beef sirloin or tenderloin, 1 lb (500 g), cut across the grain into thin, bite-sized strips

Peanuts, 2 tablespoons toasted and chopped

Fresh basil, preferably Thai, ¼ cup (⅓ oz/10 g) slivered

Steamed rice, for serving

SERVES 4

1 Make the sauce
In a small bowl, stir together the coconut milk, fish sauce, brown sugar, and lime juice.

2 Stir-fry the vegetables
Heat a wok or large frying pan over high heat until very hot and add 2 tablespoons of the oil. Add the onion and bell pepper and stir-fry just until tender, about 3 minutes. Using a slotted spoon, transfer to a bowl.

3 Cook the beef
Return the pan to high heat and add the remaining 2 tablespoons oil. Add the red curry paste and stir-fry until fragrant, about 1 minute. Stir in the sauce, bring to a gentle boil, adjust the heat to maintain a gentle boil, and cook until the sauce begins to thicken, 5–7 minutes. Return the vegetables to the pan, stir in the beef, and simmer just until the beef is cooked through, about 2 minutes. Transfer to a serving bowl, garnish with the peanuts and basil, and serve with the rice.

cook's tip

Serve the shrimp with a citrus-
soy dipping sauce: stir together
3 tablespoons fresh lemon
juice, 2 tablespoons soy sauce,
1 tablespoon water, ½ teaspoon
minced fresh cilantro (fresh
coriander), ¼ teaspoon sugar,
and 1 clove garlic, minced. The
dipping sauce may be made
a day in advance, covered, and
refrigerated; bring to room
temperature before serving.

salt & pepper shrimp

1 Make the spice mixture
In a small bowl, stir together the sugar, five-spice powder, and ¼ teaspoon each salt and pepper.

2 Sear the shrimp
Heat a wok or large frying pan over high heat until very hot and add 2 tablespoons of the oil. Meanwhile, spread the cornstarch on a plate. Quickly pat the shrimp dry and dip each shrimp into the cornstarch, coating both sides and shaking off the excess. Add the shrimp to the pan in a single layer and sear, turning once, just until opaque throughout, about 1 minute on each side. Using a slotted spoon, transfer the shrimp to a bowl.

3 Finish the dish
Return the pan to high heat and add the remaining 2 tablespoons oil. Add the ginger, garlic, and chile and stir-fry for about 5 seconds until fragrant. Add the spice mixture and mirin, quickly return the shrimp to the pan, and stir-fry until the shrimp are coated with the spice mixture and are heated through, 15–20 seconds. Serve with the dipping sauce (see Cook's Tip, left).

Sugar, ¼ teaspoon

Chinese five-spice powder, ¼ teaspoon

Salt and freshly ground pepper

Corn or peanut oil, 4 tablespoons (2 fl oz/60 ml)

Cornstarch (cornflour), ¼ cup (1 oz/30 g)

Large shrimp (prawns), 1½ lb (750 g), peeled and deveined

Ginger, 2 tablespoons minced

Garlic, 3 cloves, minced

Red or green jalapeño chile, 1, seeded and minced

Mirin, 2 tablespoons

SERVES 4

spring vegetable stir-fry

Asparagus, ½ lb (250 g), ends trimmed and cut into bite-sized pieces

Sugar snap peas, ½ lb (250 g), trimmed

Frozen petite peas, 1 cup (5 oz/155 g)

Hoisin sauce, 1 tablespoon

Soy sauce, 1 tablespoon

Rice vinegar, 1 tablespoon

Asian sesame oil, 1 teaspoon

Cornstarch (cornflour), ½ teaspoon

Corn or peanut oil, 2 tablespoons

Leek, 1, white part only, halved, rinsed, and thinly sliced

Ginger, 1 tablespoon minced

Steamed rice, for serving

SERVES 4

1 Parboil the vegetables

Bring a large pot of water to a boil. Add the asparagus and sugar snap peas and cook for 2 minutes. About 10 seconds before draining, add the frozen peas to cook them briefly. Drain the vegetables in a colander.

2 Make the sauce

In a small bowl, combine ¼ cup (2 fl oz/60 ml) water and the hoisin sauce, soy sauce, rice vinegar, sesame oil, and cornstarch and stir to dissolve the cornstarch.

3 Stir-fry the vegetables

Heat a wok or large frying pan over high heat until very hot and add 1 tablespoon of the corn oil. Add the leek and ginger and stir-fry until the leek is tender, about 2 minutes. Add the remaining 1 tablespoon corn oil, stir in the asparagus, sugar snap peas, and peas, and continue to stir-fry until heated through, about 2 minutes. Stir in the sauce and stir until the sauce thickens, about 1 minute. Serve with the rice.

cook's tip

To remove the tough, woody ends
of the asparagus, grasp each spear
near the cut end with both hands
and bend it until it snaps. It will
break naturally at the point where
the fibrous, inedible portion starts.
Use a sharp paring knife to cut
the spears into pieces as needed.

cook's tip

Any firm white-fleshed fish, such as cod or halibut, may be substituted for the sea bass. Before cooking, quickly check for errant

bones by running your fingers lightly over the edge of each fillet. If you detect any bones, remove them with needle-nosed pliers or a paring knife, pulling them straight out to avoid tearing the fish.

sea bass with ginger & green onions

1 **Make the sauce**
Preheat the oven to 425°F (220°C). In a small bowl, combine 3 tablespoons water and the soy sauce, oyster sauce, sesame oil, corn oil, sugar, cornstarch, and a pinch of white pepper and stir well to dissolve the sugar and cornstarch.

2 **Cook the sea bass**
Place the fish in a baking dish just large enough to accommodate the fillets in a single layer without crowding. Scatter the green onions and ginger over the fillets and then evenly pour the sauce over the fish. Cover with aluminum foil, securing well on all sides. Place in the oven and cook until opaque throughout when tested with the tip of a knife, 12–15 minutes.

3 **Garnish and serve**
Remove from the oven and then carefully remove the foil. Spoon the pan juices over the fillets, garnish with the cilantro, and serve directly from the dish with the rice.

Soy sauce, 2 tablespoons

Oyster sauce, 1 tablespoon

Asian sesame oil, 1 tablespoon

Corn or peanut oil, 1 teaspoon

Sugar, ½ teaspoon

Cornstarch (cornflour), ¼ teaspoon

White pepper

Sea bass fillets, 4, about 1½ lb (750) total weight

Green (spring) onions, 3, thinly sliced

Ginger, 2 tablespoons thinly sliced strips

Fresh cilantro (fresh coriander), 3 tablespoons chopped

Steamed rice, for serving

SERVES 4

45

30 minutes
start to finish

caramelized halibut with bok choy

Asian fish sauce,
⅓ cup (3 fl oz/80 ml)

Soy sauce, 2 tablespoons

Sugar, ¾ cup (6 oz/185 g)

Corn or peanut oil,
2 tablespoons

Shallots, 3, thinly sliced

Ginger, 2 tablespoons grated

Garlic, 2 cloves, minced

Freshly ground pepper

Halibut or cod fillets,
4, 1½ lb (750 g) total weight,
each 1 inch (2.5 cm) thick

Bok choy, ½ lb (250 g),
quartered lengthwise

**Fresh cilantro (fresh
coriander),** 2 tablespoons
leaves

Steamed rice, for serving

SERVES 4

1 Make the sauce
In a small bowl, stir together 3 tablespoons warm water, the fish sauce, and the soy sauce. In a small, heavy saucepan over medium heat, combine the sugar and 2 tablespoons water and stir until the sugar dissolves. Raise the heat to high, stop stirring, and instead swirl the pan until the sugar syrup turns light amber, 3–5 minutes. Remove from the heat and carefully pour the fish sauce mixture into the syrup. It will bubble and spatter. Stir until the bubbling subsides. Set aside.

2 Braise the fish
Heat a Dutch oven or large frying pan over high heat until very hot and add the oil. Add the shallots, ginger, and garlic and sauté until tender, about 2 minutes. Season with ¼ teaspoon of pepper and stir in the sauce. Reduce the heat to low, place the fish in the liquid, cover, and braise for 7 minutes. Using a metal spatula, carefully turn the fillets, lay the bok choy quarters around them, re-cover, and continue to braise until the fish is opaque throughout when tested with the tip of a knife, about 7 minutes longer. Transfer the fish to a serving platter, spoon the sauce over the top, garnish with the cilantro, and serve with the rice.

cook's tip

You may make the sauce up to 5 days in advance. Let cool then transfer to an airtight container and refrigerate until needed. Stir the sauce into the shallot mixture just before you add the fish.

cook's tip

If you cannot find Asian eggplants, you can use a globe eggplant of the same weight. Because larger eggplants are sometimes

bitter and have a higher water content, it is a good idea to salt them to draw out the bitterness and excess moisture. Toss the cubed eggplant with about 1 tablespoon salt, place in a colander, and let stand for about 15 minutes. Pat dry before stir-frying.

eggplant, portobello & chicken stir-fry

1 Make the sauce

In a bowl, combine 2 tablespoons water and the soy sauce, Worcestershire sauce, tomato paste, sesame oil, sugar, and cornstarch and stir to dissolve the sugar and cornstarch.

2 Stir-fry the chicken and vegetables

Heat a wok or large nonstick frying pan over high heat until very hot and add 2 tablespoons of the corn oil. Add the chicken and stir-fry until opaque throughout, about 2 minutes. Using a slotted spoon, transfer the chicken to a bowl. Return the pan to high heat and add the remaining 2 tablespoons corn oil. Add the eggplant and stir-fry until crisp and golden brown, about 7 minutes. Add the ginger, garlic, and mushrooms and continue to stir-fry until the mushrooms have released much of their liquid, about 3 minutes longer. Return the chicken to the pan. Give the sauce a quick stir, add to the pan, and stir until the sauce thickens slightly, 1–2 minutes. Serve with the rice.

Soy sauce, 2 tablespoons

Worcestershire sauce, 2 tablespoons

Tomato paste or ketchup, 1 teaspoon

Asian sesame oil, 1 teaspoon

Sugar, 1 teaspoon

Cornstarch (cornflour), ¼ teaspoon

Corn or peanut oil, 4 tablespoons (2 fl oz/60 ml)

Skinless, boneless chicken breasts or thighs, ½ lb (250 g), cut into bite-sized cubes

Asian eggplants (slender aubergines), 3, about 1 lb (500 g) total weight, cut into bite-sized cubes

Ginger, 1 tablespoon grated

Garlic, 1 clove, minced

Portobello or cremini mushrooms, ¼ lb (125 g), stems discarded and caps cut into bite-sized pieces

Steamed rice, for serving

SERVES 4

vietnamese beef noodle salad

Garlic, 6 cloves, minced

Unsweetened coconut milk, ½ cup (4 fl oz/125 ml)

Asian fish sauce, ½ cup (4 fl oz/125 ml)

Light brown sugar, 2 tablespoons plus 1½ teaspoons firmly packed

Sirloin or flank steak, 1, 1 lb (500 g) and about 1½ inches (4 cm) thick

Dried rice vermicelli or rice stick noodles, 6 oz (185 g), soaked in hot water for 15 minutes and drained

Fresh lime juice, from 2 limes

Corn or peanut oil, 6 tablespoons (3 fl oz/90 ml)

Shallots, 3, thinly sliced

Red or green jalapeño chile, 1, seeded and thinly sliced

Fresh basil, preferably Thai, ½ cup (¾ oz/20 g) slivered

Fresh mint, ¼ cup (⅓ oz/ 10 g) slivered

SERVES 4

1 Marinate the steak and prepare the grill

In a shallow dish, combine half of the garlic, the coconut milk, ¼ cup (2 fl oz/60 ml) of the fish sauce, and the 2 tablespoons brown sugar and stir to dissolve the sugar. Add the steak, turn to coat, cover, and let stand for 20 minutes. Prepare a gas or charcoal grill for direct grilling over high heat.

2 Make the salad

Meanwhile, bring a large pot of water to a boil. Plunge the vermicelli into the water and boil for just 5 seconds. Drain immediately but do not rinse, and place in a large bowl. In a blender, combine the remaining garlic, the remaining ¼ cup fish sauce, the 1½ teaspoons brown sugar, the lime juice, and 5 tablespoons (2½ fl oz/75 ml) of the oil and process until smooth to make the dressing. Scatter the shallots, chile, basil, and mint over the noodles, drizzle with the dressing, and toss to mix well. Set aside.

3 Grill the beef

Remove the steak from the marinade, discard the marinade, and pat the steak dry. Lightly oil the grill rack with the remaining tablespoon of oil, and place the steak on the grill. Cook, turning once, until well browned on both sides and medium-rare at the center, 4–5 minutes on each side. Transfer to a cutting board and let rest for 2 minutes. Thinly slice across the grain, capturing any juices. Arrange the slices on top of the salad, drizzle with the juices, and serve.

cook's tip

Rice noodle salad, called *bun* in Vietnamese, often includes cucumber, bean sprouts, and other crunchy vegetables. Add ¼ cup (1 oz/30 g) each thinly sliced cucumber, bean sprouts, shredded carrot, and shredded lettuce to the salad for more flavor. To save time, grill the steak in a stove-top grill pan. Preheat over high heat, brush with oil, and use the same timing.

beef & broccoli

1 Make the sauce
In a bowl, combine ⅓ cup (3 fl oz/80 ml) water and the oyster sauce, soy sauce, wine, sesame oil, cornstarch, sugar, and a pinch of pepper and stir to dissolve the cornstarch and sugar.

2 Cook the broccoli and the noodles
Bring a large pot of water to a boil. Add the broccoli and cook until tender-crisp, 3–4 minutes. Using a slotted spoon, transfer the broccoli to a colander and rinse with cold running water to halt the cooking. Return the water to a boil, add the noodles, and cook, stirring occasionally, just until tender, about 1 minute. Drain the noodles and toss with 1 tablespoon of the corn oil. Transfer to a large bowl or platter and cover loosely with aluminum foil to keep warm.

3 Stir-fry the beef and broccoli
Heat a wok or large frying pan over high heat until very hot and add the remaining 2 tablespoons corn oil. Add the ginger and stir-fry until golden brown, about 1 minute. Using the slotted spoon, scoop out and discard the ginger. Add the beef to the seasoned oil and stir-fry just until browned, about 2 minutes. Using the slotted spoon, transfer the beef to a bowl. Return the pan to high heat, add the reserved sauce, and cook, stirring, until slightly thickened, about 30 seconds. Return the beef to the pan, add the broccoli, and stir-fry until heated through, about 1 minute. Spoon over the noodles and serve.

Oyster sauce, ¼ cup (2 fl oz/60 ml)

Soy sauce, 3 tablespoons

Rice wine or dry sherry, 2 tablespoons

Asian sesame oil, 2 teaspoons

Cornstarch (cornflour), 1 teaspoon

Sugar, ½ teaspoon

White or freshly ground black pepper

Broccoli, 1 bunch, ½ lb (250 g), cut into florets

Fresh Chinese egg noodles, ½ lb (250 g)

Corn or peanut oil, 3 tablespoons

Ginger, 3 thin slices

Sirloin or flank steak, 1 lb (500 g), thinly sliced against the grain into strips

SERVES 4

lemongrass pork stir-fry

Lemongrass, 4 stalks

Garlic, 6 cloves, chopped

Fresh cilantro (fresh coriander), 4 tablespoons chopped

Freshly ground pepper

Pork loin, 3 lb (1.5 kg) cut into bite-sized cubes

Fresh lemon juice, from 1 lemon

Asian fish sauce, 2 tablespoons

Brown sugar, 2 teaspoons firmly packed

Corn or peanut oil, 4 tablespoons (2 fl oz/60 ml)

Shallots, 6, thinly sliced

Green (spring) onions, 4, thinly sliced

Steamed rice, for serving

SERVES 4–6

1 Marinate the pork

Cut off and discard the leafy tops from each lemongrass stalk. Trim off the base of the pale, bulblike bottom part and slice very thinly. In a blender, combine the lemongrass, 4 tablespoons water, the garlic, cilantro, and ½ teaspoon pepper and process until a thick paste forms. Place the pork in a bowl, add the lemongrass mixture, and stir to coat the pork evenly. Set aside for 20 minutes.

2 Make the sauce

In a small bowl, combine 6 tablespoons water and the lemon juice, fish sauce, and brown sugar and stir to dissolve the sugar.

3 Stir-fry the pork

Heat a wok or large nonstick frying pan over high heat until very hot and add 2 tablespoons of the oil. Add the pork and cook until browned on all sides, 5–7 minutes. Using a slotted spoon, transfer the pork to a bowl. Return the pan to medium heat and add the remaining 2 tablespoons oil. Add the shallots and stir-fry until translucent, about 2 minutes. Pour the sauce into the pan, bring to a boil, and boil for 1 minute. Return the pork to the pan and stir-fry until heated through, about 1 minute longer. Garnish with the green onions, transfer to a platter, and serve with the rice.

cook's tip

Lemongrass is available at Asian markets and well-stocked grocery stores, but if you cannot find it, you can substitute lemon zest and juice. Add the finely grated zest and fresh juice from 1 lemon to the ingredients in the blender.

cook's tip

To make the soup up to a day
in advance, prepare the broth
through step 1. About 15 minutes
before serving, soak the noodles.
Just before serving, reheat the
broth and add the chicken and
noodles. You can also substitute
beef broth for the chicken broth
and ½ lb (250 g) beef sirloin, cut
into thin strips, for the chicken.
Simmer the beef for 1–2 minutes
before adding the noodles.

five-spice chicken
noodle soup

1 Prepare the broth
In a large saucepan over high heat, combine the broth, shallots, ginger, and five-spice powder and bring to a boil. Reduce the heat to low and simmer, uncovered, for 10 minutes.

2 Prepare the sauce and condiments
Squeeze the juice from 2 limes to total 3 tablespoons. In a small bowl, combine the lime juice, fish sauce, and sugar and stir to dissolve the sugar. Cut the remaining lime into wedges and place on a plate with the basil and sliced chile.

3 Season the broth and finish the soup
Pour the sauce into the simmering broth and stir in the chicken to heat through. Add the noodles to the broth to heat for about 5 seconds. Ladle into bowls, garnish with the green onions, and serve with the condiments for diners to add as desired.

Chicken broth, 6 cups (48 fl oz/1.5 l)

Shallots, 3, thinly sliced

Ginger, 2 tablespoons minced

Chinese five-spice powder, 1 teaspoon

Limes, 3

Asian fish sauce, ¼ cup (2 fl oz/60 ml)

Sugar, 2 teaspoons

Fresh basil, preferably Thai, 1 cup (1 oz/30 g) slivered

Red or green jalapeño chile, 1, thinly sliced

Cooked shredded chicken, homemade or rotisserie, 2 cups (12 oz/375 g)

Dried rice stick noodles, 6 oz (185 g), soaked in hot water for 15 minutes and drained

Green (spring) onions, 2, thinly sliced

SERVES 4

grilled hoisin pork chops & asparagus

Hoisin sauce, 3 tablespoons

Fresh orange juice,
3 tablespoons

Soy sauce, 2 tablespoons

Rice wine or dry sherry,
2 tablespoons

Brown sugar, 1 teaspoon
firmly packed

Corn or peanut oil,
2 tablespoons

Ginger, 1 tablespoon grated

Garlic, 3 cloves, minced

Pork loin chops, 4, 2 lb
(1 kg) total weight, each
1 inch (2.5 cm) thick

**Salt and freshly ground
pepper**

Asparagus, ½ lb (250 g),
ends trimmed

Steamed rice, for serving

SERVES 4

1 Prepare the grill and make the sauce

Prepare a gas or charcoal grill for direct grilling over medium-high heat. In a small bowl, combine 3 tablespoons water and the hoisin sauce, orange juice, soy sauce, wine, and brown sugar and stir to dissolve the sugar. In a small saucepan over medium heat, warm 1 tablespoon of the oil. Add the ginger and garlic and sauté for about 5 seconds until fragrant. Add the hoisin sauce mixture and simmer for about 2 minutes. Set aside half of the sauce as a glaze for the pork and asparagus. Just before serving, reheat the remaining sauce for passing at the table.

2 Grill the pork chops and asparagus

Season the pork chops on both sides with ½ teaspoon salt and ¼ teaspoon pepper. Lightly oil the grill rack with the remaining tablespoon of oil, and place the chops and asparagus on it, arranging the asparagus perpendicular to the bars (to prevent them from falling through the rack). Brush some sauce on the asparagus and then the chops and grill until well browned on the first side, 4–5 minutes. Turn the chops, rotate the asparagus, brush with more sauce, and continue to grill until well browned on the second side, 4–5 minutes longer. When tested with a knife tip, the asparagus should be just tender and the chops should be pale pink at the center. Transfer the chops and asparagus to a platter. Serve with the rice and pass the warm sauce at the table.

cook's tip

The chops and asparagus can also be cooked on a stove-top grill pan, using about the same timing. Or, you can cook the pork on the stovetop and roast the asparagus on a rimmed baking sheet. Roast the spears in a 450°F (230°C) oven for 10–15 minutes, rotating them once and brushing with the sauce.

cook's tip

Other leafy greens, such as Swiss chard, kale, or spinach, may be used in place of the bok choy. Chop the leaves coarsely and cook just until tender. The spinach only needs several seconds to cook.

braised soy-ginger chicken & bok choy

1 Braise the chicken

In a Dutch oven or deep frying pan, combine 1 1/2 cups (12 fl oz/375ml) water and the soy sauce, wine, brown sugar, five-spice powder, ginger, and green onions. Bring to a boil over high heat and then reduce the heat to medium-low. Submerge the chicken pieces, skin side up, in the liquid and simmer gently for 8 minutes. Turn the pieces and continue to simmer until the chicken is opaque throughout when tested with the tip of a knife, about 8 minutes longer.

2 Cook the bok choy

Using tongs or a slotted spoon, transfer the chicken to a serving platter and cover with aluminum foil to keep warm. Bring the braising liquid to a boil over medium heat, add the bok choy, and cook until tender, about 3 minutes. Using the tongs or slotted spoon, transfer the bok choy to the platter, arranging it around the chicken.

3 Glaze the chicken

Bring the braising liquid to a boil over high heat and boil until reduced by half, about 5 minutes. Stir in the honey and sesame oil. Pour over the chicken and bok choy and serve with the rice.

Soy sauce, 1 cup
(8 fl oz/250 ml)

Rice wine or dry sherry,
1/4 cup (2 fl oz/60 ml)

Brown sugar, 2 tablespoons
firmly packed

Chinese five-spice powder,
1/2 teaspoon

Ginger, 2 tablespoons minced

Green (spring) onions,
3, thinly sliced

**Skin-on, bone-in chicken
thighs or breast halves,**
2 lb (1 kg)

Bok choy, 1/2 lb (250 g),
quartered lengthwise

Honey, 2 tablespoons

Asian sesame oil,
1 tablespoon

Steamed rice, for serving

SERVES 4

miso-glazed scallops with asian slaw

White miso, ¼ cup
(2 oz/60 g)

Mirin or sake, ¼ cup
(2 fl oz/60 ml)

Ginger, 2 tablespoons grated

Sea scallops, 1 lb (500 g)

Rice vinegar, ¼ cup
(2 fl oz/60 ml)

Sugar, ½ teaspoon

Salt

Corn or peanut oil,
4 tablespoons (2 fl oz/60 ml)

Asian sesame oil,
1 tablespoon

Napa cabbage, 1 small head
or ½ large head, shredded

Carrots, 2, peeled and
shredded

Shallots, 2, thinly sliced

SERVES 4

1 Marinate the scallops
In a large bowl, stir together the miso, mirin, and ginger. Add the scallops and turn to coat evenly with the marinade. Set aside for 15 minutes.

2 Make the slaw
In a large bowl, whisk together the vinegar, sugar, salt, 2 tablespoons of the corn oil, and the sesame oil and stir to dissolve the sugar and salt. Add the cabbage, carrots, and shallots and toss to coat evenly with the dressing. Transfer the slaw to a platter or dinner plates and set aside.

3 Sear the scallops
Heat a large nonstick frying pan over high heat until very hot. Add the remaining corn oil to the pan. Remove the scallops from the marinade, shaking off the excess marinade, and place in a single layer in the pan. Sear until crisp and brown on the first side, about 1 minute. Using tongs, turn the scallops and sear until the second side is crisp and brown and the center springs back when touched, 1–2 minutes. Place the scallops on the slaw and serve.

cook's tip
Miso, a savory, highly nutritional fermented paste made from soybeans, comes in many colors, thicknesses, and varieties.

White miso, also known as *shiromiso,* is available in Japanese groceries, health-food stores, and well-stocked supermarkets. You may substitute sea bass fillets for the scallops, cooking them as you do the scallops or grilling them.

cook's tip

You may add meat, poultry, or seafood to this dish, such as ½ lb (250 g) pork loin or skinless, boneless chicken thighs, cut into thin strips, or peeled shrimp (prawns), chopped. Add to the pan after stir-frying the ginger and garlic and cook just until cooked through, 3–4 minutes, then proceed as directed.

vegetable
chow mein

1 Parboil the noodles and make the sauce

Bring a large pot of water to a boil. Add the noodles, boil for 2 minutes, drain into a colander, and rinse well with cold running water. Place in a bowl, add 1 tablespoon of the corn oil, and toss to coat evenly. In a small bowl, stir together 3 tablespoons water and the oyster sauce, soy sauce, vinegar, sesame oil, and sugar and stir to dissolve the sugar.

2 Stir-fry the vegetables

Heat a wok or large frying pan over high heat until very hot and add 2 tablespoons of the corn oil. Add the onion and bell pepper and stir-fry just until tender, about 2 minutes. Add the mushrooms and zucchini and continue to stir-fry until golden brown, about 2 minutes. Using a slotted spoon, transfer the vegetables to a bowl.

3 Stir-fry the noodles

Return the pan to high heat and add the remaining 2 tablespoons corn oil. Add the ginger and garlic and stir-fry for about 5 seconds until fragrant. Add the noodles and cook until heated through, about 5 minutes. Return the vegetables to the pan, add the sauce, and continue to stir and toss until all the ingredients are well combined and heated through, about 1 minute. Transfer to a platter and serve.

Fresh Chinese egg noodles, ½ lb (250 g)

Corn or peanut oil, 5 tablespoons (2½ fl oz/ 75 ml)

Oyster sauce, 2 tablespoons

Soy sauce, 2 tablespoons

Rice vinegar, 2 tablespoons

Asian sesame oil, 1 tablespoon

Sugar, 1 teaspoon (optional)

Yellow onion, ½, thinly sliced

Red bell pepper (capsicum), 1, seeded and thinly sliced lengthwise

Shiitake mushrooms, ¼ lb (125 g), stems discarded and caps thinly sliced

Zucchini (courgette), 1, trimmed and cut into matchsticks

Ginger, 1 tablespoon grated

Garlic, 2 cloves, minced

SERVES 4

thai green curry shrimp

Thai green curry paste, 1 tablespoon

Garlic, 3 cloves, coarsely chopped

Unsweetened coconut milk, 1 can (13½ fl oz/ 420 ml)

Asian fish sauce, ¼ cup (2 fl oz/60 ml)

Fresh lime juice, from 1 lime

Light brown sugar, 2 teaspoons firmly packed

Corn or peanut oil, 4 tablespoons (2 fl oz/60 ml)

Shallots, 2, thinly sliced

Zucchini (courgettes) or yellow summer squashes, ¾ lb (12 oz/375 g), trimmed, halved lengthwise, and sliced thinly crosswise

Large shrimp (prawns), 1½ lb (750 g), peeled and deveined

Fresh basil, preferably Thai, 2 tablespoons slivered

Steamed rice, for serving

SERVES 4

1 Prepare the curry base

In a blender, combine 2 tablespoons water and the curry paste and garlic and process until smooth. In a small bowl, combine the coconut milk, fish sauce, lime juice, and brown sugar and stir to dissolve the sugar.

2 Cook the curry

Heat a wok or large frying pan over high heat until very hot and add 2 tablespoons of the oil. Add the shallots and stir-fry until translucent, 1 minute. Add the zucchini and stir-fry just until it browns, 4–5 minutes. Using a slotted spoon, transfer the vegetables to a bowl. Return the pan to high heat and add the remaining 2 tablespoons oil. Add the curry paste and stir-fry for about 5 seconds until fragrant. Stir in the coconut milk mixture, reduce the heat to medium, and simmer for 5 minutes to blend the flavors. Add the shrimp and continue to simmer until the shrimp just turn opaque throughout, about 3 minutes. Spoon into a serving bowl, garnish with the basil, and serve with the rice.

cook's tip

You may substitute 2 lb (1 kg) mussels or clams for the shrimp. Scrub well, discarding any shellfish that fail to close to the touch. Pour water to a depth of ½ inch (12 mm) into a large saucepan, add the shellfish, cover, and steam until they open, about 3 minutes. Discard any that fail to open. Using a slotted spoon, transfer them to the simmering curry just before serving.

braised salmon & shiitakes

1 Prepare the braising liquid

In a large bowl, combine the chicken broth, soy sauce, wine, sugar, and cornstarch and stir to dissolve the sugar and cornstarch. In a Dutch oven or large, deep frying pan over medium heat, warm the oil. Add the ginger, garlic, and all but 1 tablespoon of the green onions and sauté until fragrant, about 5 seconds. Add the mushrooms and sauté until just beginning to brown, 2–3 minutes. Add the braising liquid, bring to a boil, and then reduce the heat to low so the liquid simmers gently.

2 Braise the fish and cook the noodles

Place the salmon steaks in the braising liquid in a single layer, cover, and cook for 5 minutes. Using a metal spatula, carefully turn the steaks, re-cover, and braise until the fish is opaque throughout when tested with the tip of a knife, about 5 minutes longer. Meanwhile, bring a large pot of water to a boil. Add the noodles and boil just until tender, 3–5 minutes. Drain into a colander and rinse under warm running water. Transfer to individual plates.

3 Serve the fish

Carefully arrange the braised fish on the noodles. Top with the thickened braising sauce, garnish with the reserved green onions, and serve.

Chicken broth, 2 cups (16 fl oz/500 ml)

Soy sauce, ½ cup (4 fl oz/125 ml)

Rice wine or dry sherry, ¼ cup (2 fl oz/60 ml)

Sugar, 1 tablespoon

Cornstarch (cornflour), 1½ teaspoons

Corn or peanut oil, 2 tablespoons

Ginger, 2 tablespoons grated

Garlic, 3 cloves, minced

Green (spring) onions, 2, thinly sliced

Shiitake mushrooms, ¼ lb (125 g), stems discarded and caps thinly sliced

Salmon steaks, 4, about 1½ lb (750 g) total weight, each 1½ inches (4 cm) thick

Fresh Chinese egg noodles, 6 oz (185 g)

SERVES 4

thai pumpkin & chicken curry

Pumpkin or butternut squash, 1 small, 1½ lb (750 g), halved, seeded, peeled, and cut into bite-sized cubes

Shallots, 2, chopped

Garlic, 3 cloves, coarsely chopped

Thai red curry paste, 1 tablespoon

Unsweetened coconut milk, 1 can (13½ fl oz/ 420 ml)

Asian fish sauce, 2 tablespoons

Fresh lime juice, from 1 lime

Light brown sugar, 2 teaspoons firmly packed

Corn or peanut oil, 3 tablespoons

Skinless, boneless chicken thighs, 1 lb (500 g), cut into bite-sized cubes

Fresh basil, preferably Thai, 2 tablespoons slivered

Steamed rice, for serving

SERVES 4

1 Cook the pumpkin
Bring a large pot of water to a boil. Add the pumpkin and boil just until barely tender, about 7 minutes. Drain well and set aside.

2 Prepare the curry base
In a blender, combine the shallots, garlic, and curry paste with 2 tablespoons water and process until smooth. In a small bowl, combine the coconut milk, fish sauce, lime juice, and sugar and stir to dissolve the sugar.

3 Cook the curry
In a wok or large frying pan over medium heat, warm 2 tablespoons of the oil. Add the chicken and sear until light brown on all sides, 5–7 minutes. Using a slotted spoon, transfer the chicken to a bowl. Return the pan to medium heat and add the remaining 1 tablespoon oil. Add the curry base and cook, stirring, for about 10 seconds until fragrant. Stir in the coconut milk mixture and bring to a boil. Add the chicken and pumpkin, reduce the heat to low, and simmer until the pumpkin is tender when pierced with a fork and the chicken is opaque throughout, about 5 minutes longer. Transfer to a serving bowl, garnish with the basil, and serve with the rice.

cook's tip

Look for small, sweet pumpkin varieties like Sugar Pie or Cheese or substitute butternut squash. To prepare the pumpkin or squash, steady it on its side on a rigid cutting surface and, using a large, sharp knife, cut it in half through the stem end. (If the peel is thick, tap the knife with a mallet.) Scoop out the seeds and fibers with a large metal spoon. Finally, peel and cut as desired.

15 minutes
hands-on time

shanghai noodles with pork

Fresh Chinese egg noodles, 1 lb (500 g)

Corn or peanut oil, 5 tablespoons (2½ fl oz/ 75 ml)

Soy sauce, ¼ cup (2 fl oz/ 60 ml)

Worcestershire sauce, 3 tablespoons

Rice vinegar, 2 tablespoons

Sugar, 1 teaspoon

White pepper

Boneless pork loin, ½ lb (250 g), cut across the grain into thin strips

Yellow onion, 1, thinly sliced

Red bell pepper (capsicum), 2, seeded and thinly sliced crosswise

Garlic, 2 cloves, minced

Napa cabbage, ½ head, finely shredded

SERVES 4

1 Parboil the noodles

Bring a large pot of water to a boil. Separate the strands of noodles, drop into the boiling water, and boil for 2 minutes. Drain into a colander and rinse with cold running water. Place in a bowl, add 1 tablespoon of the oil, and toss to coat evenly.

2 Make the sauce

In a small bowl, stir together ⅓ cup (3 fl oz/80 ml) warm water and the soy sauce, Worcestershire sauce, vinegar, sugar, and a pinch of pepper and stir to dissolve the sugar.

3 Stir-fry the pork and noodles

Heat a wok or large nonstick frying pan over high heat until very hot and add 2 tablespoons of the oil. Add the pork and stir-fry just until browned, 2–3 minutes. Using a slotted spoon, transfer the pork to a bowl. Return the pan to high heat and add the remaining 2 tablespoons oil. Add the onion and bell peppers and stir-fry just until tender, about 5 minutes. Stir in the garlic and cabbage and stir-fry until the cabbage begins to wilt, about 3 minutes. Pour in the sauce and bring to a boil. Stir in the parboiled noodles and pork and mix well with the vegetables, cover, reduce the heat to low, and cook, stirring once or twice, until the noodles have absorbed the sauce, about 10 minutes. Transfer to bowls and serve.

cook's tip

You may use ½ lb (250 g) skinless, boneless chicken breasts, cut into thin strips, or ½ lb (250 g) small shrimp (prawns), peeled and deveined, in place of the pork. Both will cook in about 8 minutes. Or, for a vegetarian dish, omit the pork and add ¼ lb (125 g) sliced shiitake mushrooms.

cook's tip

Fish sauce is a salty and pungent Asian seasoning popular in Vietnam and Thailand. The amber liquid is the filtered extract of

small fish (often anchovies), salt, and water which has been left to ferment in the sun. It is an essential seasoning in countless dishes, and used in many Asian dipping sauces.

grilled vietnamese chicken

1 Marinate the chicken

In a blender, combine the garlic, the chopped shallots, the ginger, coconut milk, 3 tablespoons of the vinegar, the fish sauce, soy sauce, and 1 tablespoon of the sugar and process until smooth. Place the chicken in a nonreactive bowl, add the marinade, stir to coat evenly, and cover with plastic wrap. Let sit for at least 15 minutes at room temperature, or for up to overnight in the refrigerator. (For the best flavor, marinate the chicken for at least 4 hours in the refrigerator.)

2 Make the cucumber salad

In a bowl, whisk together the remaining vinegar, the remaining sugar, 1 teaspoon salt, and 4 tablespoons of the oil. Add the cucumber and the sliced shallots, toss to mix, cover, and refrigerate until serving. (The salad can be made a day in advance and stored in an airtight container in the refrigerator.)

3 Grill the chicken

Prepare a gas or charcoal grill for direct grilling over medium heat and lightly oil the grill rack with the remaining 1 tablespoon oil. Remove the chicken from the marinade, shaking off the excess, and discard the marinade. Place the chicken, skin side up, on the grill rack and grill until browned, 7–8 minutes. Using tongs, turn and grill on the skin side until browned, 5–7 minutes longer. Move the chicken away from the direct heat, cover the grill, and continue to cook until opaque or an instant-read thermometer inserted into the thickest part away from bone registers 160°F (71°C), 7–10 minutes. Serve the chicken with the cucumber salad.

Garlic, 4 cloves, coarsely chopped

Shallots, 4, 2 chopped and 2 sliced

Ginger, 1 tablespoon chopped

Unsweetened coconut milk, ½ cup (4 fl oz/125 ml)

Rice vinegar, 6 tablespoons (3 fl oz/90 ml)

Asian fish sauce, 3 tablespoons

Soy sauce, 2 tablespoons

Brown sugar, 2 tablespoons firmly packed

Skin-on, bone-in chicken breast halves and/or thighs, 2 lb (1 kg)

Salt

Corn or peanut oil, 5 tablespoons (3 fl oz/80 ml)

English cucumber, 1 large, thinly sliced

SERVES 4

rice with chicken, mushrooms & chard

Skinless, boneless chicken thighs, 2, cut into bite-sized pieces

Ginger, 1 teaspoon minced

Oyster sauce, 1 tablespoon

Soy sauce, 1 tablespoon

Rice wine or dry sherry, 1 tablespoon

Asian sesame oil, 1 teaspoon

Sugar, ¼ teaspoon

White pepper

Jasmine rice, 1½ cups (10½ oz/330 g)

Swiss chard, 1 bunch, stems removed and leaves chopped

Shiitake mushrooms, 6 oz (185 g), stems discarded and caps thinly sliced

Green (spring) onion, 1, thinly sliced

SERVES 4

1 Marinate the chicken

In a large bowl, combine the chicken, ginger, oyster sauce, soy sauce, wine, oil, sugar, and a pinch of pepper and stir to mix well. Let stand for 10 minutes.

2 Cook the rice

In a heavy saucepan, combine the rice, Swiss chard, mushrooms, chicken and its marinade, and 3 cups (24 fl oz/ 750 ml) water. Bring to a boil over high heat, cover, reduce the heat to low, and cook until the rice has absorbed the water and the chicken is cooked, about 20 minutes. Remove from the heat and let stand, covered, for 10 minutes. Fluff the rice with a fork, transfer to a serving bowl, garnish with the green onion, and serve. Alternatively, this dish may be prepared in an electric rice cooker. Combine the rice, Swiss chard, mushrooms, chicken and its marinade, and 3 cups (24 fl oz/750 ml) boiling water in the rice cooker, cover, and turn on the cooker. The rice should be ready in about 30 minutes. Once the cooker goes off, let it stand undisturbed for 10 minutes before serving.

cook's tip

For added flavor, in a small bowl, stir together 2 tablespoons oyster sauce, 1 teaspoon Asian sesame oil, 1 tablespoon rice vinegar, and 1 teaspoon hot water. Drizzle over the rice before serving.

curried chickpea & potato stew

1 Prepare the curry base

In a blender, combine 1 tablespoon water with the onion, ginger, garlic, and chile and process until a paste forms. In a small bowl, stir together the curry powder and ½ teaspoon salt.

2 Sauté the vegetables

Heat a large frying pan over high heat until very hot and add 2 tablespoons of the oil. Add the potatoes and sauté until lightly browned, about 5 minutes. Season with ¼ teaspoon salt and, using a slotted spoon, transfer to a bowl. Return the pan to high heat and add 1 tablespoon of the oil. Add the okra, if using, and sauté until slightly crisp, about 5 minutes. Using the slotted spoon, transfer the okra to the bowl with the potatoes.

3 Cook the stew

Return the pan to medium-high heat and add the remaining 1 tablespoon oil. Add the onion-garlic paste and fry until fragrant, about 2 minutes. Stir in the curry powder and broth, mix well, and bring to a boil. Return the vegetables to the pan and add the chickpeas. Reduce the heat to low and cook, uncovered, until the potatoes are tender, 15–20 minutes. Taste and adjust the seasoning with salt. Serve with the rice.

Yellow onion, 1, coarsely chopped

Ginger, 2 tablespoons chopped

Garlic, 4 cloves, chopped

Red or green jalapeño chile, 1 small, seeded and chopped

Curry powder, 1½ tablespoons

Salt

Corn or peanut oil, 4 tablespoons (2 fl oz/60 ml)

Boiling potatoes, 2 large, peeled and cut into small cubes

Okra, ½ lb (250 g), fresh or frozen, trimmed and thickly sliced (optional)

Chicken or vegetable broth, 1½ cups (12 fl oz/ 375 ml)

Chickpeas (garbanzo beans), 1 can (14½ oz/ 455 g), drained and rinsed

Steamed rice, for serving

SERVES 4

83

roasted honey-soy pork tenderloin

Ginger, 1 tablespoon chopped

Garlic, 3 cloves, chopped

Hoisin sauce, 2 tablespoons

Soy sauce, 2 tablespoons

Rice wine or dry sherry, 1 tablespoon

Ketchup, 1 tablespoon

Honey, 1 ½ tablespoons

Corn or peanut oil, 1 tablespoon

Asian sesame oil, 1 ½ teaspoons

Pork tenderloin, 1, about 1 lb (500 g)

SERVES 4

1 **Marinate the pork tenderloin**
In a blender, combine the ginger, garlic, hoisin sauce, soy sauce, wine, ketchup, honey, corn oil, and sesame oil and process until smooth. Place the tenderloin in a shallow baking dish, add the marinade, turn the pork to coat evenly, and cover with plastic wrap. Let sit for 15 minutes at room temperature. (For the best flavor, marinate for at least 4 hours and up to overnight in the refrigerator.)

2 **Roast the tenderloin**
Preheat the oven 400°F (200°C). Place a wire rack in a roasting pan just large enough to accommodate the tenderloin. Remove the pork from the marinade and place on the rack. Reserve the marinade. Roast the pork for 20 minutes. Remove from the oven, brush the pork on all sides with the marinade, and return to the oven. Continue to roast until the exterior is crisp and brown and an instant-read thermometer inserted into the thickest part of the tenderloin registers 145°–150°F (60°–65°C), 10–15 minutes longer. Let rest for 10 minutes, then slice and serve.

cook's tip

Use any leftover pork you
might have to make a pork and
vegetable chow mein. Slice the
pork into thin strips and follow
the Vegetable Chow Mein recipe
on page 67. Add pork along
with the noodles in step 3.

cook's tip

Good-quality canned coconut milk is available in Asian markets and many supermarkets. The solids in coconut milk separate and rise to the top, forming a thick creamlike layer, so shake the can well before using. Don't buy canned sweetened coconut cream, which is used for tropical drinks and some desserts.

curried cauliflower & chicken stew

1 Prepare the aromatics and spice mixture
In a blender, combine 1 tablespoon water and the onion, ginger, and garlic and process until a paste forms. In a small bowl, stir together the curry powder and ½ teaspoon salt.

2 Cook the chicken
Heat a large frying pan over high heat until very hot and add the oil. Add the onion-garlic paste and sauté just until it begins to brown, about 5 minutes. Stir in the spice mixture and sauté for about 10 seconds until fragrant. Add the tomatoes and cook, stirring occasionally, until they begin to break down, about 5 minutes. Stir in the coconut milk and ½ cup (4 fl oz/ 125 ml) water, bring to a simmer, and stir in the chicken pieces. Cover, reduce the heat to low, and simmer until the stew thickens, about 20 minutes.

3 Cook the vegetables
Uncover and stir in the cauliflower and green beans. Re-cover and continue to cook until the vegetables are tender, 15–20 minutes. Season to taste with salt. Serve with the rice.

Yellow onion, 1 small, coarsely chopped

Ginger, 2 tablespoons chopped

Garlic, 3 cloves, chopped

Curry powder, 1 tablespoon

Salt

Corn or peanut oil, 2 tablespoons

Tomatoes, ¾ lb (375 g), seeded and chopped

Unsweetened coconut milk, 1 can (13½ fl oz/ 420ml)

Skinless, boneless chicken thighs, 1 lb (500 g), cut into large cubes

Cauliflower, 1 small head, cut into florets

Green beans, ¼ lb (125 g), trimmed and cut into 2-inch (5-cm) pieces

Steamed rice, for serving

SERVES 4

yellow chicken curry

Skin-on, bone-in chicken breasts and/or thighs, 2 lb (1 kg)

Salt

Corn or peanut oil, 2 tablespoons

Yellow onion, 1, chopped

Ginger, 1 tablespoon minced

Garlic, 3 cloves, minced

Curry powder, 1½ tablespoons

Unsweetened coconut milk, 1 can (13½ fl oz/ 420 ml)

Fresh lemon juice, from 1 lemon

Boiling potatoes, 2 large, peeled and cut into large cubes

Carrots, 2, peeled and cut into large pieces

Steamed rice, for serving

SERVES 4

1 Brown the chicken

Sprinkle the chicken pieces evenly with 1 teaspoon salt. Heat a Dutch oven or large ovenproof frying pan over high heat until very hot and add the oil. Add the chicken, skin side down, and sear until crisp and brown, 5–6 minutes. Turn the pieces and sear on the other side, 5–6 minutes longer. Using tongs or a slotted spoon, transfer the chicken to a plate.

2 Make the curry

Preheat the oven to 325°F (165°C). Return the pan to high heat, add the onion, ginger, and garlic, and sauté until just tender, about 2 minutes. Stir in the curry powder and sauté 10 seconds longer. Add the coconut milk, ½ cup (4 fl oz/ 125 ml) water, the lemon juice, and 1 teaspoon salt. Bring to a boil, return the chicken pieces to the pan, and simmer for 2 minutes. Cover tightly, transfer to the oven, and cook for 30 minutes. Remove from the oven, stir in the potatoes and carrots, re-cover, return to the oven, and continue to cook until the potatoes and carrots are tender, about 30 minutes longer. Uncover and cook for a final 10 minutes to allow the curry to thicken. Serve with the rice.

cook's tip

For a quicker version of this curry, substitute a rotisserie chicken for the chicken pieces. Starting with step 2, proceed with the recipe as directed, simmering the potatoes and carrots in the curry until tender, about 40 minutes. During the last 10 minutes of cooking, add the chicken pieces.

cook's tip

For a heartier dish, stir in ½ lb
(250 g) boiling potatoes, peeled
and cut into large cubes, during
the last 20 minutes of cooking.
The stew may be prepared up to
2 days in advance, covered, and
refrigerated; reheat over medium-
low heat just before serving. It can
also be frozen for up to 2 months.

indian
braised lamb

1 Prepare the aromatics and spice mixture
In a blender, combine the onion, ginger, garlic, and chile and process until a paste forms. In a small bowl, stir together the coriander, curry powder, and cinnamon.

2 Sear the lamb
Season the lamb with 1 teaspoon salt. Heat a Dutch oven or large, deep frying pan over high heat until very hot and add 2 tablespoons of the oil. Add the lamb in a single layer, working in batches if necessary to avoid crowding, and sear, turning once, until browned on all sides, 8–10 minutes. Using a slotted spoon, transfer the lamb to a plate.

3 Braise the lamb
Return the pan to medium heat and add the remaining 1 tablespoon oil. Add the onion-garlic paste and sauté just until it begins to brown, about 3 minutes. Stir in the spice mixture and sauté 10 seconds longer. Add 2 cups (16 fl oz/500 ml) water and 1 teaspoon salt. Bring to a boil over medium-high heat and then reduce the heat to low. Gradually whisk in the yogurt until combined with the sauce. Return the lamb to the pan, cover, and simmer gently until the lamb is tender, 60–70 minutes. Taste and adjust the seasoning with salt. Serve with the rice.

Yellow onion, 1, chopped

Ginger, 2 tablespoons chopped

Garlic, 3 cloves, chopped

Red or green jalapeño chile, 1 small, seeded and minced

Ground coriander, 1 tablespoon

Curry powder, 1 teaspoon

Ground cinnamon, 1/4 teaspoon

Boneless lamb shoulder, 2 lb (1 kg), cut into large cubes

Salt

Corn or peanut oil, 3 tablespoons

Plain yogurt, 1 cup (12 oz/ 375 g)

Steamed rice, for serving

SERVES 4

sichuan braised pork with eggplant

Corn or peanut oil,
4 tablespoons (2 fl oz/60 ml)

Boneless pork shoulder,
1 ½ lb (750 g), cut into
large cubes

Soy sauce, ⅓ cup (3 fl oz/
80 ml)

Rice wine or dry sherry,
¼ cup (2 fl oz/60 ml)

Brown sugar, 2 tablespoons
firmly packed

Chinese five-spice powder,
1 teaspoon

Cornstarch (cornflour),
½ teaspoon

**Asian eggplants (slender
aubergines),** ½ lb (250 g),
cut into cubes

Ginger, 4 thin slices

Green (spring) onions,
2, thinly sliced

Garlic, 4 cloves, minced

Steamed rice, for serving

SERVES 4

1 Sear the pork

Heat a Dutch oven or large, deep frying pan over high heat until very hot and add 2 tablespoons of the oil. Add the pork in a single layer and sear, turning once, until golden brown on all sides, 8–10 minutes. Using a slotted spoon, transfer the pork to a plate.

2 Braise the pork and eggplant

In a large bowl, stir together 2 cups (16 fl oz/500 ml) water and the soy sauce, wine, brown sugar, five-spice powder, and cornstarch. Return the pan to high heat and add the remaining 2 tablespoons oil. Add the eggplants and sauté until lightly browned and just beginning to soften, about 5 minutes. Using the slotted spoon, transfer the eggplant to a bowl. Return the pan to medium heat, add the ginger, 3 tablespoons of the green onions, and the garlic, and sauté for about 10 seconds until fragrant. Pour in the soy sauce mixture, bring to a boil, and stir in the seared pork. Cover, reduce the heat to low, and cook until the pork is tender, 60–70 minutes. Uncover, add the reserved eggplant, and simmer until the eggplant is tender and the flavors are blended, 10–15 minutes. Transfer to a serving bowl, garnish with the remaining green onions, and serve with the steamed rice.

cook's tip

Eggplants come in myriad sizes, shapes, and colors, but the most common type available is the globe eggplant, which is usually

large and pear shaped with thin, purple-black skin. Asian eggplants, which are often smaller and more slender, are deep purple, lavender, and sometimes white. In both cases, look for specimens that feel firm and heavy for their size, have smooth, shiny skin, and are free of bruises.

the smarter cook

Adding Asian dishes to your weekday menus is a good way to put delicious, satisfying meals on the table that don't take a lot of time and work. From Chinese stir-fries and Indian curries to Vietnamese salads, the bright flavors and quick-cooking methods of Asia's kitchens are a boon to the busy home cook.

Most of the recipes in this book take no more than 30 minutes from pantry to table, especially if you stick to a few simple rules. Keep your pantry well stocked and you will always have the basics for your weekday dinners. Draw up a weekly menu plan and a detailed shopping list and you will make fewer—and briefer—trips to the store. In the following pages, you will find scores of tips on how to organize your time, stock your kitchen, and create easy and delicious menus, all keys to becoming a smarter cook.

get started

Careful planning and organization are the keys to becoming a smarter cook who turns out wonderful Asian dinners without having to spend long hours in the kitchen or at the store. Three simple strategies will ease the way: putting together a weekly menu plan, preparing a shopping list, and stocking your kitchen with basic Asian ingredients (pages 105 and 106).

plan an asian meal

To make the most of your time, map out your menus in advance (see the sample menus on page 98 for ideas). Choose your recipes carefully, taking the season and your schedule into consideration.

■ **Plan for the whole week.** On the weekend, take time to think about the week ahead. A good strategy for time-saving is to include at least one recipe that can be easily doubled, such as a soup or curry, and then splitting it over two nonsuccessive nights or freezing one batch for a future meal. Also, vary the types of recipes you select, serving a stir-fry one night and a grilled dish on another night.

■ **Match menus to fit your schedule.** Once you know your weekly commitments, you can pick main dishes that fit comfortably into the time you have each night. If possible, prepare components of some dishes ahead on the weekend or on evenings when you have free time.

■ **Follow the seasons.** Vegetables and fruits at the peak of their season have more flavor, cost less, and add seasonal variety to your cooking (see right). Seafood dishes, salads and chilled noodles are perfect for hot-weather dining, while hearty stews and curries are welcome when it is cold outside.

■ **Involve everyone.** Ask family members for their suggestions when planning your weekly menu. They will become more interested in trying new dishes and enjoy each meal more. Enlist their help when it is time to prepare dinner, too. Encourage them to stir soups and sauces, wash and chop vegetables, or set the table.

THINK SEASONALLY

Using seasonal vegetables guarantees dishes with great flavors every time you cook. Use this guide to match recipes with the best each season has to offer.

spring Prepare light main courses, salads, and soups that highlight baby greens, asparagus, fresh herbs (such as mint and cilantro/fresh coriander), leeks, green (spring) onions, new potatoes, and sugar snap peas.

summer Use your grill to prepare seafood, poultry, or meats and serve with the season's abundant bell peppers (capsicums), eggplants (aubergines), cucumbers, green beans, basil, greens (such as arugula/rocket and spinach), snow peas (mangetouts), tomatoes, and zucchini (courgettes).

autumn Incorporate the best of the harvest in your menus, including broccoli, leeks, mushrooms, onions, potatoes, pumpkins, and yams.

winter Serve stews, curries, and braises that bring out the flavor of butternut squash, cabbage, carrots, cauliflower, Chinese broccoli, hearty greens (such as Swiss chard), and sweet potatoes.

round it out

Many Asian main dishes need no more than rice or noodles to make a complete meal. Other times, you will want to serve a vegetable side dish, salad, or soup. Here are some suggestions to help you assemble easy menus.

rice For coconut rice, substitute unsweetened coconut milk for one-fourth of the cooking liquid. For herbed rice, fold chopped fresh Thai basil, mint, or cilantro (fresh coriander) into hot rice. For lemon rice, stir fresh lemon juice, melted unsalted butter, and a pinch of salt into hot rice. For spiced rice, cook rice with 1 tablespoon unsalted butter and 3 fresh ginger slices, 2 whole cloves, a few cumin seeds, or 1 cinnamon stick.

steamed or boiled vegetables Steam or boil sturdy vegetables, such as asparagus, broccoli, carrots, green beans, and cauliflower for serving at room temperature. Drizzle with soy sauce, a few drops of Asian sesame oil, or corn or peanut oil heated with a few cumin seeds or some orange zest. Sprinkle with chopped cashews or toasted sesame seeds.

grilled vegetables Brush thickly sliced Asian eggplants (slender aubergines), halved small zucchini (courgettes), or fresh shiitake mushrooms with oil, sprinkle with salt, and cook on a stove-top grill pan or in the broiler (grill). Serve with lemon wedges.

lightly pickled vegetables Immerse beans sprouts in hot salted water for about 10 minutes, drain, and season with rice vinegar, sugar, and chopped green (spring) onion. Or, toss cucumber slices with rice vinegar, soy sauce, sugar, and thinly sliced red onion.

caramelized vegetables Sauté diced winter squash, eggplant (aubergine), or sliced fresh mushrooms in oil with minced ginger until golden. Mix equal parts soy sauce, brown sugar, and rice vinegar; stir into vegetables; and reduce to a glaze.

stir-fried greens Stir-fry thinly sliced garlic in oil until crisp and golden. Add dark, leafy greens, such as spinach, watercress, Chinese broccoli, or bok choy, drizzle in a small amount of broth, and stir-fry until tender. Finish with Asian sesame oil, salt, and pepper.

chicken salad Bone and skin rotisserie chicken and tear into strips. Toss with shredded napa cabbage, shredded carrot, and sliced red onion. Toss with a soy sauce dressing and toasted sesame seeds.

noodle salad Boil soba or egg noodles and stir in finely shredded cabbage and shredded carrots just before draining. Toss with bottled sesame or peanut dressing and sprinkle with chopped green (spring) onion or chopped fresh cilantro (fresh coriander).

watercress salad In a large bowl, whisk together peanut or corn oil, rice vinegar or fresh lemon juice, a few drops Asian sesame oil, salt, and freshly ground pepper. Add watercress sprigs, tomato wedges, and thinly sliced hard-boiled eggs and toss gently.

drinks Infuse lemonade or iced tea with bruised lemongrass stalks or ginger slices. Garnish ginger ale with mint sprigs and lime slices. Blend together 1 cup plain yogurt and 1 mango, thinning with water as needed, for a quick *lassi* to accompany Indian dishes.

desserts Seasonal fruits, such as oranges, pineapple, or persimmons, are the best finale to an Asian meal. For a special treat, top ginger ice cream with mango slices, layer Ruby grapefruit and tangerine segments with lime sorbet in a parfait glass, or serve sautéed banana slices with pound cake and coconut ice cream.

sample meals

IN MINUTES meals highlight recipes that go together quickly and easily. FIT FOR COMPANY menus are special-occasion meals that don't require spending hours in the kitchen.

IN MINUTES	FIT FOR COMPANY
Beef with Ginger & Caramelized Onions (page 14) Stir-fried asparagus with soy sauce Steamed rice	**Roasted Honey-Soy Pork Tenderloin** (page 84) Ginger-glazed butternut squash Fresh Chinese egg noodles with soy sauce
Chile-Garlic Prawns (page 22) Stir-fried sugar snap peas with green onion Fresh Chinese egg noodles	**Seared Salmon with Basil** (page 29) Stir-fried zucchini & squash matchsticks Lemon rice
Japanese Pork Katsu (page 34) Shredded cabbage salad with rice wine vinaigrette Steamed rice	**Indian Braised Lamb** (page 91) Sautéed cauliflower Basmati rice with cilantro
Cashew Chicken (page 10) Steamed broccoli with sesame seeds Steamed rice	**Thai Green Curry Shrimp** (page 68) Cucumber & red onion salad with rice wine vinaigrette Steamed rice
Sea Bass with Ginger & Green Onions (page 45) Steamed bok choy Steamed rice	**Grilled Vietnamese Chicken** (page 79) Roasted eggplant with soy sauce & basil Herbed rice

SHORTCUT INGREDIENTS

Supermarkets offer a growing selection of convenient Asian ingredients in their international food aisles. Also look for other items, such as those listed below, that help save time in the kitchen.

precut vegetables Many produce sections offer bags of precut vegetables, including special mixes that are ideal for Asian dishes. Look for cubes of winter squash for curries; sliced cabbage coleslaw mix for slaw and noodle dishes; and sliced bell peppers (capsicums), broccoli florets, and sliced mushrooms for stir-fries.

prewashed greens Buy salad greens, baby spinach, and arugula (rocket) for tossed salads and mustard greens and spinach for quick stir-fries.

prepared sauces Time-saving sesame sauces, peanut sauces, and soy sauce–based dressings are easy to incorporate into recipes. On labels look for minimal additives in ingredient lists. Once home, adjust the seasonings of the bottled sauces with your own favorite flavors.

precut meats Purchasing chicken tenders, cubed pork, and sliced beef streamlines preparation time in the kitchen. Alternatively, buy a large cut of meat and ask your butcher to slice it thinly for you. At home, divide the slices into practical portion sizes and freeze for future meals, saving both time and money. Tender meat from the loin is ideal for quick cooking, while cuts from the tougher shoulder or leg require longer cooking.

shop smarter

For flavorful, healthful meals, always select the freshest seasonal produce and other ingredients of the highest-quality you can find. Although the recipes in this book call for items that you will typically find in most supermarkets, a visit to an Asian market, a good butcher shop or fishmonger, or other specialty store will offer a wider selection and more authentic flavors.

■ **Produce** If you live or work near a farmers' market, try to visit it regularly for the best seasonal produce. Choose vegetables and fruits that are heavy for their size and avoid those with bruises or dried, discolored stems. The leaves of greens and herbs should be crisp and bright colored. Potatoes, zucchini (courgettes), eggplants (aubergines), and onions should have smooth, taut skins and dense, firm flesh. Whenever possible, avoid out-of-season or imported produce, which is often picked long before it is ripe to survive shipping and is usually more expensive and less flavorful than regionally grown produce.

■ **Meat & poultry** When purchasing packaged meat or poultry, choose packages free of any liquid. Meats should have a uniform color, a firm texture, and a fresh smell. The fat should be white, not gray, and any bones should look moist. Poultry should be plump, with smooth skin and firm flesh, and any visible fat should be white to light yellow. If you're making a recipe that calls for boned meat or poultry, ask the butcher to do it for you to save you time in the kitchen.

■ **Fish & shellfish** Always purchase seafood from a trusted source, as it is highly perishable, and ask which items in the case are freshest. Look for bright color, a moist, smooth surface, and a firm texture. Avoid any fish that holds an imprint when pressed with a fingertip, and pass up any fish or shellfish that has an off odor. Plan carefully so that you use seafood the same day you purchase it.

■ **Broth & stock** Good-quality broths can be found in cans and aseptic boxes in the soup aisle of most supermarkets. On labels look for short ingredients lists that include minimal additives. Some specialty markets also offer their own made-from-scratch fresh or frozen broths.

MAKE A SHOPPING LIST

prepare in advance Create your shopping list after planning your weekly menu. Review the recipes while you assemble the list, so you know what you will need. Check the pantry and add any items to the list that need restocking to make the meals on your menus.

create a template Make a shopping list template on your computer. It will not only smooth the process and establish an organized ritual, but will also allow you to review, change, or share the list easily.

use categories Divide your list into the same sections as your regular supermarket, such as produce; meat and seafood; dairy; and pantry items. You will save time walking the aisles and, when needed, you can split the list with other family members for quicker shopping.

be flexible Be ready to change your menus based on the freshest ingredients you find at the market.

save your lists Label the shopping lists that include your favorite recipes and then file them away for use again in the future, shaving off even more time during the planning phase.

tools & techniques

Asian cuisines don't require lots of special gadgets, but having a handful of everyday tools in your kitchen will help get meals on the table quickly and easily. Since cleaning any equipment can also take time, choose mechanical shortcuts wisely. Having good-quality, versatile tools and mastering a handful of basic techniques are investments that return hours of saved time in the kitchen.

time-saving tools

- **Blender** A blender makes quick work of mixing aromatic ingredients into a thick paste or smooth liquid. When blending nearly dry mixtures, add a small amount of water or oil to help the blades spin freely.

- **Food processor** A food processor is handy for puréeing and for slicing and grating vegetables. A model with a capacity of 4 cups (32 fl oz/1 l) or less is handy for mixing sauces and marinades.

- **Kitchen shears** Fresh herbs, green (spring) onions, chiles, and dried mushrooms are just a few of the ingredients that can be snipped quickly and cleanly with kitchen shears. Heavy-duty shears with a notched blade can even handle harder vegetables and small bones.

- **Mandoline** Made up of a long, rectangular frame, a cutting blade with a plain and a serrated edge, and a guiding plate, this easy-to-use tool uniformly slices vegetables and fruits with a sweep of the hand. French-fry and julienne blades are also available.

- **Rasp grater** Resembling a long file with a sturdy handle and razor-sharp cutters, this stainless-steel tool quickly and easily grates fresh ginger and citrus zest.

- **Rice cooker** This countertop electric appliance cooks steamed rice conveniently and consistently. You can choose from simple one-button models to more advanced cookers that allow you to customize for specific types of rice, schedule time-delay cooking, or even remember the exact texture you like for your cooked rice. Some models easily convert to steamers for cooking vegetables.

CHOOSING A PAN

wok A large wok, at least 14 inches (35 cm) in diameter, is ideal for stir-frying, as its deep bowl shape offers plenty of room for stirring and helps concentrate the high heat required for quick cooking. A wok with a nonstick surface requires less oil and is easy to clean. A spun-steel wok, the traditional choice, should be seasoned before its first use (see right). Avoid washing your wok with soap to preserve the natural oil coating that develops over time.

frying pan Any wide, deep frying pan can be used for stir-frying. Pans with a thick, heavy bottom will sear ingredients more evenly and maintain high heat better as you add ingredients.

dutch oven A large, heavy, round or oval pot with a lid and heatproof loop handle ensures low, uniform heat for flavorful, tender stews and curries cooked on the stove top or in the oven.

pot A large pot is essential for cooking noodles. Look for a pot with both a strainer insert for draining noodles easily and a perforated insert that allows the pot to double as a steamer, thus making use of the same boiling water twice.

A staple in Asian cooking, long-grain rice, such as jasmine and basmati, cooks up to a dry, light texture, while medium- and short-grain rices, popular with Japanese dishes, are softer and moister. Avoid parboiled, or converted, rice, as it lacks the proper texture and flavor for serving with Asian dishes.

The exact ratio of water to rice varies with different types of rice, but here are general directions for cooking rice on the stove top: For 3 cups (15 oz/470 g) cooked rice, place 1 cup (7 oz/220 g) rice in a fine-mesh sieve and rinse until the water runs clear. Transfer the rice to a heavy saucepan and add 1½ cups (12 fl oz/375 ml) water. Bring to a boil, give the rice a quick stir, reduce the heat to low, cover, and cook, undisturbed, for 20 minutes. Let rest, covered, off the heat for 10 minutes, then fluff before serving. Cook twice as much rice as you need for a meal and refrigerate the extra for up to 2 days or freeze for up to 1 month.

SEASONING YOUR WOK

Seasoning seals your wok so that food doesn't stick to the surface. To season a new wok, clean it with warm water and mild soap, then place it over medium heat to warm. Moisten a paper towel with canola or other mild oil and rub it over the surface of the wok. Turn the heat to low and heat for 15 minutes.

basic techniques

■ **Cutting vegetables** Ingredients cut into similar shapes and sizes are ideal for the short cooking times and high heat of stir-frying. Have all the vegetables for a recipe ready before you start cooking. Cut them into bite-sized pieces, taking into account that the denser a vegetable is, the more time it will take to cook through. Thin, diagonal slices maximize surface area, reducing cooking time while adding visual appeal.

■ **Juicing citrus** Oranges, lemons, and limes are easier to squeeze and give more juice when they are at room temperature. If you store them in the refrigerator, microwave them for about 20 seconds before juicing. They will also release more juice if you first roll them firmly on a countertop to soften their inner membranes.

■ **Slicing meat** For stir-frying, cut meat across the grain into very thin slices for both tenderness and quick cooking. For easier slicing, freeze meat for about 30 minutes to firm it up, or ask your butcher to slice the meat when you purchase it.

■ **Preheating pans** Be sure your wok or frying pan is hot before adding seafood, poultry, meats, or vegetables. A cool pan will extend the cooking time and compromise the texture of the final dish.

■ **Thickening with cornstarch** Adding a little cornstarch (cornflour) dissolved in cold liquid (1 part cornstarch to 4 parts liquid) to the liquid in a pan creates a smooth, translucent sauce. Generally, 1 teaspoon cornstarch will thicken 1 cup (8 fl oz/250 ml) simmering liquid to a medium-bodied sauce. To prevent lumps, always use cold liquid, and always stir the mixture to recombine just before adding to the pan. Do not boil for more than 5 minutes, or the cornstarch will begin breaking down and the sauce will thin again.

■ **Reheating rice** To reheat leftover rice that has been stored in the refrigerator or freezer (see Cooking Rice, left), place it in a rice cooker or in a steamer or saucepan on the stove top, sprinkle with a small amount of water, cover, and heat until hot. Or, place in a bowl, moisten lightly, and heat in the microwave for 1 to 2 minutes, stirring once.

the well-stocked kitchen

Smart cooking is all about being prepared. Keeping your
pantry, refrigerator, and freezer well stocked and organized will
save you time, giving you a head start when you are ready
to cook dinner. Keeping track of what is on your shelves and
shopping with a carefully assembled shopping list means
fewer trips to the store and less time in the aisles.

On the pages that follow, you will find a guide to selecting
and storing the ingredients you will need to make the quick
and tasty Asian recipes in this book. You will also find dozens
of good ideas on how to keep foods fresh, maintain your
pantry, and shop efficiently. Take some time now to organize
your kitchen and stock your shelves, and you will able to make
any dish in this book by picking up no more than a handful
of fresh ingredients at the store.

the pantry

Your pantry is wherever you store your dried, canned, and jarred foods and such fresh ingredients as onions, garlic, and shallots that do not require refrigeration. It is typically cupboards or a closet and should be dry and dark and away from the heat of the stove. It should also be well organized, so that you can quickly locate whatever ingredients you need in the rush of weeknight cooking.

stock your pantry

- **Take inventory.** Remove all the items from your pantry and sort them by type, using the Pantry Staples list (see right).

- **Start clean.** Wipe the shelves with a damp cloth and reline them with fresh shelf paper, if needed.

- **Check freshness.** Look for expiration dates on all items. Discard those past their dates, and make a note of those nearing expiration. Write the date of purchase on new packages without expiration dates.

- **Make a list.** Write down items that you need to replace or restock.

- **Organize your shelves.** Return the items to the shelves, again grouping them by type and keeping the items you use most often toward the front. To keep oils, vinegars, and spices fresh and flavorful as long as possible, store them in airtight containers in the darkest, coolest part of the pantry.

keep it organized

- **Check your staples.** As you plan your weekly menu, check your pantry to make sure you have all the ingredients you will need.

- **Keep a list.** Regularly check the ingredients in your pantry and add depleted staples to your weekly shopping list.

- **Rotate items.** Place newly purchased ingredients toward the back of the shelves, moving older items to the front where they will be used first.

ASIAN INGREDIENTS

Most of the ingredients in this book are readily available in any supermarket, but you may not recognize a few items. Look for the following in well-stocked supermarkets or Asian grocery stores.

curry paste a prepared Thai curry base; often in red or green

fish sauce a salty, pungent seasoning made from anchovies, salt, and water

hoisin sauce a sweet, tangy sauce made from fermented soybeans

five-spice powder a spice mix usually containing cinnamon, star anise, fennel, Sichuan pepper, and cloves

mirin sweet rice cooking wine

SPICES

Spices start losing their flavor after about 6 months, so purchase them in small quantities. Many markets now carry spices in the bulk-foods section, which means you can buy only as much as you will use in the near future.

PANTRY STORAGE

rice & dried noodles Store rice in airtight containers for up to 3 months, checking occasionally for signs of rancidity or infestation. The shelf life of most dried noodles is 1 year. Although they are safe to eat beyond that time, they will have lost flavor and can become brittle. Once you break the seal on a package, slip what you don't cook into a resealable storage bag or an airtight container and return to the shelf.

oils Store unopened bottles of oil at room temperature in a cool, dark place. Although oils will keep for up to 1 year, their flavor diminishes over time. Once a bottle is opened, store for 3 months at room temperature or in the refrigerator for several months. Taste or smell oils to make sure they are not rancid before using them.

fresh pantry foods Check your fresh pantry items—citrus fruits, garlic, onions, shallots, and some roots and tubers—occasionally for sprouting or spoilage and discard if necessary. Never put potatoes alongside onions; when placed next to each other, they produce gases that hasten spoilage.

canned foods Discard canned foods if the can shows any signs of expansion or buckling. Once you have opened a can, transfer the unused contents to an airtight container and refrigerate or freeze.

dried herbs Buy dried herbs in small quantities, store in airtight containers, and use within 6 months, after which they will have lost their potency.

PANTRY STAPLES

RICE & NOODLES
cellophane noodles
egg noodles, thick
egg noodles, thin
long-grain rice
rice noodles, thin
rice noodles, wide
rice vermicelli

SPICES
black peppercorns
curry powder
five-spice powder
ground cinnamon
ground coriander
salt

OILS & VINEGARS
Asian sesame oil
corn or peanut oil
rice vinegar

SAUCES & FLAVORINGS
chile sauce (Sriracha)
curry paste, green
curry paste, red
fish sauce
hoisin sauce
hot mustard
ketchup
oyster sauce
soy sauce
tomato paste
Worcestershire sauce

SWEETENERS
honey
sugar, brown
sugar, granulated

SPIRITS
dry sherry
mirin
rice wine
sake

CANNED FOODS
chicken broth
chickpeas (garbanzo beans)
coconut milk, unsweetened

FRESH FOODS
garlic
ginger
limes
potatoes
shallots
tomatoes
yellow onions

MISCELLANEOUS
bread crumbs, dried
cornstarch (cornflour)
flour
panko (Japanese bread crumbs)
peanut butter, creamy
roasted cashews
roasted peanuts
sesame seeds
shiitake mushrooms, dried

the refrigerator & freezer

A refrigerator and a freezer stocked with a dependable selection of good-quality ingredients are essential to a well-organized kitchen. The refrigerator is ideal for keeping fresh produce, meats, poultry, and seafood, as well as some leftovers. The freezer will preserve most of the flavor and nutrients of some foods, such as shrimp (prawns), and is recommended for storing some finished dishes, such as soups and curries.

general tips

- Foods lose flavor under refrigeration, so proper storage and an even temperature of below 40°F (5°C) are important.

- Freeze foods at 0°F (-18°C) or below to retain color, texture, and flavor.

- Don't crowd foods in the refrigerator or freezer. Air should circulate freely to keep foods evenly cooled.

- To prevent freezer burn, use only airtight containers, resealable plastic bags, or moistureproof wrappings, such as aluminum foil.

leftover storage

- Most stir-fries, curries, and soups can be stored in the refrigerator for up to 4 days or in the freezer for up to 2 months.

- Let food cool to room temperature before refrigerating or freezing. Transfer the cooled food to an airtight plastic or glass container, leaving room for expansion if freezing. Or, put the cooled food into a resealable plastic freezer bag, expelling as much air as possible before sealing.

- Plan on freezing some soups and curries in small batches for when you need to heat up just enough for 1 or 2 servings. Remember to allow headspace, as they will expand as they freeze.

- Thaw frozen foods overnight in the refrigerator or quickly in the microwave. To avoid bacterial contamination, never thaw foods, particularly meats or poultry, at room temperature.

COLD STORAGE STAPLES

Keep most of these everyday ingredients on hand not only for making Asian dishes, but for all kinds of cooking. When you're ready to make any recipe in this book, you will need to buy only a few fresh produce, meat, or poultry items. Replace these staples as needed, always rotating the oldest items to the front of the shelf as you restock.

PRODUCE

basil, Thai

carrots

fresh cilantro (fresh coriander)

green (spring) onions

jalapeño chiles

DAIRY

eggs

plain yogurt

MISCELLANEOUS

firm tofu

white miso

FROZEN

petite peas

shrimp (prawns), peeled

fresh herb & vegetable storage

- To keep cilantro (fresh coriander) fresh, trim off the stem ends, stand the bunch in a glass of water, drape a plastic bag loosely over the leaves, and place in the refrigerator. Wrap other fresh herbs in a damp paper towel, place in a plastic bag, and store in the crisper. Rinse and stem all herbs just before using.

- Rinse leafy greens, such as spinach or Swiss chard, spin dry in a salad spinner, wrap in damp paper towels, and store in a resealable plastic bag in the crisper.

- In general, store other vegetables in plastic bags in the crisper and rinse just before using. Sturdy vegetables will keep for up to 1 week, while more delicate ones will keep for only a few days.

- Store tomatoes and eggplants (aubergines) at room temperature in a cool, dry location.

- Trim the stem ends of asparagus spears, stand the spears upright in a container of water, and store in the refrigerator for up to 1 week.

- To prevent bruising, store delicate produce, such as herbs and salad greens, in an area of the refrigerator separate from heavy vegetables, such as carrots, cabbage, or green beans.

meat, poultry & seafood storage

- Seafood is highly perishable, so keep it refrigerated at all times until ready to use and always try to cook it the same day you purchase it. If using mussels or clams, place in a bowl, cover with a damp kitchen towel, and use within a day.

- Place packaged meats or poultry on a large plate or tray in the coldest part of the refrigerator and use within 2 days of purchase.

- If you do not use all the meat or poultry in a package, discard the original wrapping and rewrap what remains in fresh wrapping. Return to the refrigerator or freeze for later use.

index

A

Asparagus
  Grilled Hoisin Pork Chops and
    Asparagus, 60
  preparing, 43
  Spring Vegetable Stir-Fry, 42
  storing, 107

B

Beans
  Curried Cauliflower and Chicken
    Stew, 87
  Curried Chickpea and Potato Stew, 83
  Dry-Fried String Beans with Pork, 13
Beef
  Beef and Broccoli, 55
  Beef Sukiyaki with Noodles, 17
  Beef with Ginger and Caramelized
    Onions, 14
  Five-Spice Beef Noodle Soup, 58
  precut, 98
  shopping for, 99
  slicing thinly, 16, 101
  storing, 107
  Tangerine Beef and Snow Peas, 26
  Thai Red Curry Beef, 38
  Vietnamese Beef Noodle Salad, 52
Bell peppers
  Chicken Chow Mein, 66
  Pork Chow Mein, 66
  Shanghai Noodles with Chicken, 77
  Shanghai Noodles with Pork, 76
  Shanghai Noodles with Shrimp, 77
  Shrimp Chow Mein, 66
  Thai Red Curry Beef, 38
  Vegetable Chow Mein, 67

Blenders, 100
Bok choy
  Braised Soy-Ginger Chicken and Bok
    Choy, 63
  Caramelized Halibut with Bok Choy, 48
Braised Salmon and Shiitakes, 71
Braised Soy-Ginger Chicken and Bok
  Choy, 63
Braised Soy-Ginger Chicken and
  Greens, 62
Broccoli
  Beef and Broccoli, 55
Broths, 99, 107

C

Cabbage
  Beef Sukiyaki with Noodles, 17
  Miso-Glazed Scallops with Asian
    Slaw, 64
  Shanghai Noodles with Chicken, 77
  Shanghai Noodles with Pork, 76
  Shanghai Noodles with Shrimp, 77
  Shredded Cabbage Salad, 35
Canned foods, 105
Caramelized Halibut with Bok Choy, 48
Carrots
  Miso-Glazed Scallops with Asian
    Slaw, 64
  Yellow Chicken Curry, 88
Cashew Chicken, 10
Cauliflower and Chicken Stew, Curried, 87
Chicken
  Braised Soy-Ginger Chicken and Bok
    Choy, 63
  Cashew Chicken, 10
  Chicken Chow Mein, 66

Chicken Salad, 97
Chicken with Peanut Sauce, 21
Curried Cauliflower and Chicken
  Stew, 87
Eggplant, Portobello, and Chicken
  Stir-Fry, 51
Five-Spice Chicken Noodle Soup, 59
Grilled Vietnamese Chicken, 79
precut, 98
Rice with Chicken, Mushrooms, and
  Chard, 80
Shanghai Noodles with Chicken, 77
shopping for, 99
storing, 107
Thai Pumpkin and Chicken Curry, 72
Yellow Chicken Curry, 88
Chickpea and Potato Stew, Curried, 83
Chile-Garlic Prawns, 22
Chow mein
  Chicken Chow Mein, 66
  Pork Chow Mein, 66
  Shrimp Chow Mein, 66
  Vegetable Chow Mein, 67
Cilantro, 107
Citrus fruits
  Citrus-Soy Dipping Sauce, 40
  juicing, 101
Clams
  shopping for, 99
  Thai Green Curry Clams, 69
Coconut milk
  freezing, 107
  shopping for, 86
Cod
  Caramelized Cod with Bok Choy, 48
  Cod with Ginger and Green Onions, 44

Cornstarch, thickening with, 101

Crab Fried Rice, 25

Cucumber Salad, 79

Curries
  Curried Cauliflower and Chicken
    Stew, 87
  Curried Chickpea and Potato Stew, 83
  Thai Butternut Squash and Chicken
    Curry, 72
  Thai Green Curry Shrimp, 68
  Thai Pumpkin and Chicken Curry, 72
  Thai Red Curry Beef, 38
  Yellow Chicken Curry, 88

Curry paste, 104

D

Desserts, 97

Drinks, 97

Dry-Fried String Beans with Pork, 13

Dutch ovens, 100

E

Eggplant
  Eggplant, Portobello, and Chicken
    Stir-Fry, 51
  salting, 50
  shopping for, 93, 99
  Sichuan Braised Pork with Eggplant, 92
  storing, 107
  types of, 93

Equipment, 100

F

Fish
  Braised Salmon and Shiitakes, 71
  Caramelized Cod with Bok Choy, 48

Caramelized Halibut with Bok Choy, 48

Cod with Ginger and Green Onions, 44

frozen, 107

Halibut with Ginger and Green
    Onions, 44

Sea Bass with Ginger and Green
    Onions, 45

Seared Salmon with Basil, 29

Sesame-Crusted Tuna with Greens, 18

shopping for, 99

Sweet and Sour Panfried Sole, 37

Fish sauce, 78, 104

Five-Spice Beef Noodle Soup, 58

Five-Spice Chicken Noodle Soup, 59

Five-spice powder, 104

Food processors, 100

Freezing tips, 106–7

Fried Rice, Crab, 25

Fruits. See also individual fruits
  desserts, 97
  shopping for, 99
  storing, 105

Frying pans
  preheating, 101
  types of, 100

G

Ginger
  freezing, 107
  preparing, 15
  shopping for, 15

Graters, 100

Green beans
  Curried Cauliflower and Chicken
    Stew, 87
  Dry-Fried String Beans with Pork, 13

Greens. See also individual greens
  Braised Soy-Ginger Chicken and
    Greens, 62
  prewashed, 98
  Sesame-Crusted Tuna with Greens, 18
  storing, 107

Grilled Hoisin Pork Chops and
  Asparagus, 60

Grilled Vietnamese Chicken, 79

H

Halibut
  Caramelized Halibut with Bok Choy, 48
  Halibut with Ginger and Green
    Onions, 44

Herbs
  dried, 105
  fresh, 107

Hoisin Pork Chops and Asparagus,
  Grilled, 60

Hoisin sauce, 104

Hot and Sour Soup with Pork, 33

J

Japanese Pork Katsu, 34

K

Kale, Braised Soy-Ginger Chicken and, 62

L

Lamb, Indian Braised, 91

Lemongrass
  Lemongrass Pork Stir-Fry, 56
  substitute for, 57

Lemons, 101

Limes, 101

M

Mandolines, 100

Meat. *See also individual meats*
  precut, 98
  shopping for, 99
  slicing, 16, 101
  storing, 107

Menu planning, 96–98

Mirin, 104

Miso
  Miso-Glazed Scallops with Asian
    Slaw, 64
  varieties of, 65

Mushrooms
  Beef Sukiyaki with Noodles, 17
  Braised Salmon and Shiitakes, 71
  Chicken Chow Mein, 66
  Eggplant, Portobello, and Chicken
    Stir-Fry, 51
  Hot and Sour Soup with Pork, 33
  Pork Chow Mein, 66
  Rice with Chicken, Mushrooms, and
    Chard, 80
  Shrimp Chow Mein, 66
  Vegetable Chow Mein, 67

Mussels
  shopping for, 99
  Thai Green Curry Mussels, 69

N

Noodles
  Beef and Broccoli, 55
  Beef Sukiyaki with Noodles, 17
  Braised Salmon and Shiitakes, 71
  Chicken Chow Mein, 66
  Chicken with Peanut Sauce, 21
  Five-Spice Beef Noodle Soup, 58
  Five-Spice Chicken Noodle Soup, 59
  Noodle Salad, 97
  as pantry staples, 105
  Pork Chow Mein, 66

reconstituting dried, 20
  Shanghai Noodles with Chicken, 77
  Shanghai Noodles with Pork, 76
  Shanghai Noodles with Shrimp, 77
  Shrimp Chow Mein, 66
  storing, 105
  Vegetable Chow Mein, 67
  Vietnamese Beef Noodle Salad, 52

O

Oils, 105

Okra
  Curried Chickpea and Potato Stew, 83

Onions
  Beef with Ginger and Caramelized
    Onions, 14
  storing, 105

Oranges, 101

P

Panko, 36

Pans
  preheating, 101
  types of, 100

Pantry
  organizing, 104
  stocking, 104, 105
  storage tips for, 105

Peanut Sauce, Chicken with, 21

Peas
  Crab Fried Rice, 25
  Spicy Tofu with Peas, 30
  Spring Vegetable Stir-Fry, 42
  Tangerine Beef and Snow Peas, 26

Planning, 96–98

Pork
  Dry-Fried String Beans with Pork, 13
  Grilled Hoisin Pork Chops and
    Asparagus, 60
  Hot and Sour Soup with Pork, 33
  Japanese Pork Katsu, 34

Lemongrass Pork Stir-Fry, 56
  Pork Chow Mein, 66
  precut, 98
  Roasted Honey-Soy Pork Tenderloin, 84
  Shanghai Noodles with Pork, 76
  shopping for, 99
  Sichuan Braised Pork with Eggplant, 92
  storing, 107

Potatoes
  Curried Chickpea and Potato Stew, 83
  Indian Braised Lamb, 90
  shopping for, 99
  storing, 105
  Yellow Chicken Curry, 88

Pots, 100

Prawns. *See* Shrimp and prawns

Pumpkin and Chicken Curry, Thai, 72

R

Rasp graters, 100

Refrigerating tips, 106–7

Rice
  cooking, 101
  Crab Fried Rice, 25
  jasmine, 27
  as pantry staple, 105
  reheating, 101
  Rice with Chicken, Mushrooms, and
    Chard, 80
  rounding out meal with, 97

Rice cookers, 100

Roasted Honey-Soy Pork Tenderloin, 84

S

Salads
  Chicken Salad, 97
  Cucumber Salad, 79
  Miso-Glazed Scallops with Asian
    Slaw, 64
  Noodle Salad, 97
  Sesame-Crusted Tuna with Greens, 18

Shredded Cabbage Salad, 35
Vietnamese Beef Noodle Salad, 52
Salmon
    Braised Salmon and Shiitakes, 71
    Seared Salmon with Basil, 29
Salt and Pepper Shrimp, 41
Sauces
    Citrus-Soy Dipping Sauce, 40
    fish, 78, 104
    hoisin, 104
    as pantry staples, 105
    Peanut Sauce, 21
    prepared, 98
    thickening, 101
Scallops
    Miso-Glazed Scallops with Asian
      Slaw, 64
    shopping for, 99
Sea Bass with Ginger and Green
    Onions, 45
Seafood. See also individual seafood
    frozen, 107
    shopping for, 99
    storing, 107
Seared Salmon with Basil, 29
Seasons, cooking with, 96
Sesame-Crusted Tuna with Greens, 18
Shanghai Noodles with Chicken, 77
Shanghai Noodles with Pork, 76
Shanghai Noodles with Shrimp, 77
Shears, 100
Shopping, 99
Shredded Cabbage Salad, 35
Shrimp and prawns
    Chile-Garlic Prawns, 22
    frozen, 107
    Salt and Pepper Shrimp, 41
    Shanghai Noodles with Shrimp, 77
    shopping for, 99
    Shrimp Chow Mein, 66
    Thai Green Curry Shrimp, 68

Sichuan Braised Pork with Eggplant, 92
Slaw, Asian, Miso-Glazed Scallops with, 64
Snow Peas, Tangerine Beef and, 26
Sole, Sweet and Sour Panfried, 37
Soups
    Five-Spice Beef Noodle Soup, 58
    Five-Spice Chicken Noodle Soup, 59
    Hot and Sour Soup with Pork, 33
Spices, 104, 105
Spicy Tofu with Peas, 30
Spinach
    Braised Soy-Ginger Chicken and
      Spinach, 62
    Chicken with Peanut Sauce, 21
Spirits, 105
Spring Vegetable Stir-Fry, 42
Squash
    Thai Butternut Squash and Chicken
      Curry, 72
    Thai Green Curry Shrimp, 68
Stocks, 99
Storage tips
    for canned foods, 105
    for herbs, 105, 107
    for meat, 107
    for oils, 105
    for poultry, 107
    for rice and noodles, 105
    for seafood, 107
    for spices, 105
    for vegetables, 105, 107
Sugar snap peas
    as simple side dish, 23
    Spring Vegetable Stir-Fry, 42
Sukiyaki, Beef, with Noodles, 17
Sweet and Sour Panfried Sole, 37
Swiss chard
    Braised Soy-Ginger Chicken and Swiss
      Chard, 62
    Rice with Chicken, Mushrooms, and
      Chard, 80

T
Tangerine Beef and Snow Peas, 26
Techniques, 101
Thai Butternut Squash and Chicken
    Curry, 72
Thai Green Curry Shrimp, 68
Thai Pumpkin and Chicken Curry, 72
Thai Red Curry Beef, 38
Tofu
    Spicy Tofu with Peas, 30
    types of, 31
Tomatoes
    Curried Cauliflower and Chicken
      Stew, 87
    storing, 107
Tools, 100
Tuna, Sesame-Crusted, with Greens, 18

V
Vegetables. See also individual vegetables
    boiled, 97
    caramelized, 97
    cutting, 101
    frozen, 107
    grilled, 97
    pickled, 97
    precut, 98
    rounding out meal with, 97
    shopping for, 99
    Spring Vegetable Stir-Fry, 42
    steamed, 97
    storing, 105, 107
    Vegetable Chow Mein, 67
Vietnamese Beef Noodle Salad, 52
Vietnamese Chicken, Grilled, 79
Vinegars, 105

W
Woks
    about, 100
    seasoning, 101

Oxmoor House

OXMOOR HOUSE

Oxmoor House books are distributed by Sunset Books
80 Willow Road, Menlo Park, CA 94025
Telephone: 650 321 3600 Fax: 650 324 1532

Vice President/General Manager Rich Smeby
National Accounts Manager/Special Sales Brad Moses
Oxmoor House and Sunset Books are divisions of
Southern Progress Corporation

WILLIAMS-SONOMA
Founder & Vice-Chairman Chuck Williams

THE WILLIAMS-SONOMA FOOD MADE FAST SERIES
Conceived and produced by Weldon Owen Inc.
814 Montgomery Street, San Francisco, CA 94133
Telephone: 415 291 0100 Fax: 415 291 8841

In collaboration with Williams-Sonoma, Inc.
3250 Van Ness Avenue, San Francisco, CA 94109

Photographer Bill Bettencourt
Food Stylist Kevin Crafts
Photographer's Assistant Angelica Cao
Food Stylist's Assistant Alexa Hyman
Text Writer Thy Tran

Library of Congress Cataloging-in-Publication data is available.
ISBN-13: 978-0-8487-3148-9
ISBN-10: 0-8487-3148-4

WELDON OWEN INC.

Chief Executive Officer John Owen
President and Chief Operating Officer Terry Newell
Chief Financial Officer Christine E. Munson
Vice President International Sales Stuart Laurence
Vice President and Creative Director Gaye Allen
Vice President and Publisher Hannah Rahill
Art Director Kyrie Forbes Panton
Senior Editor Kim Goodfriend
Editor Emily Miller
Designer and Photo Director Andrea Stephany
Assistant Editor Juli Vendzules
Production Director Chris Hemesath
Color Manager Teri Bell
Production and Reprint Coordinator Todd Rechner

A WELDON OWEN PRODUCTION
Copyright © 2007 by Weldon Owen Inc. and Williams-Sonoma, Inc.
All rights reserved, including the right of reproduction in
whole or in part in any form.

Set in Formata
First printed in 2006
10 9 8 7 6 5 4 3 2 1
Color separations by Bright Arts Singapore
Printed by Tien Wah Press

Printed in Singapore

ACKNOWLEDGMENTS
Weldon Owen wishes to thank the following people for their generous support in producing this book:
Heather Belt, Ken DellaPenta, Judith Dunham, Marianne Mitten, Sharon Silva, and Jason Wheeler.

A NOTE ON WEIGHTS AND MEASURES
All recipes include customary U.S. and metric measurements. Metric conversions are based on
a standard developed for these books and have been rounded off. Actual weights may vary.